D0502337

A PILOT'S TRUE STORY

FLIGHT TO HEAVEN

A PLANE CRASH . . . A LONE SURVIVOR . . . A JOURNEY TO HEAVEN— AND BACK

CAPT. DALE BLACK

Written in collaboration with Ken Gire

MJF BOOKS
New York

Published by MJF Books
Fine Communications
322 Eighth Avenue
New York, NY 10001

Flight to Heaven
LC Control Number: 2014942387
ISBN 978-1-60671-274-0

Copyright © 2010 by Dale Black

Written in collaboration with Ken Gire

All scripture quotations are from the New King James Version
of the Bible. Copyright © 1979, 1980, 1982 by Thomas Nelson, Inc.
Used by permission. All rights reserved.

Some names of persons in this account have been changed to
protect their privacy. Some aircraft numbers have also been changed.

This edition is published by MJF Books in arrangement with Bethany
House Publishers, a division of Baker Publishing Group.

All rights reserved. No part of this publication may be reproduced or
transmitted in any form or by any means, electronic or mechanical, including
photocopy, recording, or any information storage and retrieval system,
without the prior written permission of the publisher.

Printed in the United States of America.

MJF Books and the MJF colophon are trademarks of Fine Creative Media, Inc.

QF   10   9   8   7   6   5   4   3   2

This book is dedicated to my wife, Paula,
whom I love and adore, cherish, and respect.
Without her gentle and loving prodding,
you would not be reading about my journey to heaven
or be holding this book in your hands.

IN LOVING MEMORY OF
my grandfather Russell L. Price,
a man who learned to walk by faith and not by sight.

CONTENTS

ACKNOWLEDGMENTS

After spending four years writing this book and another two years getting the help needed to bring it to fruition, the credit for the final product is broad based.

The largest thanks goes to the most important person in making this book become reality, my best friend and wife of almost forty years, Paula Black. My love and appreciation also go to my children, Eric and Kara, for enriching my life in so many ways.

I wish to thank author Beverly Swerling Martin, my writing coach, for her invaluable guidance and editing of this project. Much thanks to Lela Gilbert for helping write an earlier manuscript and to Greg Johnson, my literary agent, who believed in this project from the outset and quickly arranged the details for publication. Thank you to Kyle Duncan for being such an instrumental and effective liaison for this project with Bethany House Publishers and embracing it with his heart. Thanks go to Jeff Braun for his strategic suggestions, editing, and invaluable help in bringing this book to completion. A huge thank-you mixed with awe goes to Ken Gire, a writer with amazing skill and talent, who contributed his abilities to enhance the story in major ways.

A big thank-you for her tireless and encouraging work as my personal editor goes to Sandi Gregston. Also thanks to Ray Gregston, Dana McCue, and Nicole Elliott for their suggestions and editing of the earlier manuscript.

Thanks also to Harold Morby, a veteran of sixty years of professional photography, for taking and providing the aerial photos of the crash site.

Thanks to my sweet mother, Joyce Black, for her contagious upbeat attitude, her unending love, and for blessing her family with songs of praise throughout a lifetime.

Lastly, I wish to thank and recognize a loyal and loving friend, Kara Joy Black, the best daughter any father ever had. Kara has developed wisdom well beyond her years and I found myself seeking her counsel regularly in preparing this book.

PROLOGUE

My life was forever changed after a plane crash.

I was the only survivor.

For days I remained in an intensive care unit, but not before taking an uncharted trip . . . to heaven. What I experienced there, words cannot do justice. Even the best words pale before the indescribable. For many months following the crash, due to serious amnesia, I remembered nothing. Nothing of the crash, the first three days in the hospital, or my visit to heaven. At least, my *mind* did not remember. My heart? Well, that's a different story.

I was assigned to Dr. Homer Graham, best known as Evel Knievel's surgeon. My injuries were massive, but when I awoke in the ICU, I was a changed man. Yet I had no memory as to why. It seemed as if I had been given new eyes. I felt as though I were looking into another dimension. That was forty years ago.

What you're about to read is how my life was turned upside down by an airplane crash and why every major decision I've made since then has been a direct result of my journey to heaven. Those who know me may now understand why I've seemed like a bit of a misfit and why my life has often followed an offbeat path.

You'll learn why I've been emboldened and compelled to share the love of God with others. Why I volunteered on almost a thousand flights to more than fifty countries, building churches, orphanages, and medical clinics. And why I've trained lay ministers and medical personnel to help the needy worldwide, usually at my own expense.

Since that fateful day, I have shared my story about the crash and the amazing recovery many times. But I have never shared publicly about my journey to heaven, until now.

How could I keep this life-changing event a secret? There are several reasons.

Right after the crash my memory was like a jigsaw puzzle with only a few recognizable pieces. It would take eight months to start getting my memory back. And even longer for my injured mind and my transformed heart to get in sync.

As soon as my memory returned, I told my grandfather everything that had happened, but he cautioned me about telling others. "Dale," he said, "you can speak about your experience, or you can treat it as sacred and let your life be a reflection of your experience. By that I mean, if you really did see the other side, then live out whatever you believe you saw. Live what you believe you heard. Just live what you learned. Your life's actions will speak louder than your voice."

So I made a solemn promise to myself and to God not to share my experience with anyone until He made it clear to do so. At the time I figured God might want me to keep the secret for only a year or two.

Soon after the crash I attended a church service where a man claimed to have died, visited heaven, and come back to life. To me, the service was more self-serving than sacred. The very essence of heaven is God, yet the people were more interested in the sensation rather than the One who created it all and Whom heaven is all about. I was grieved by the event and my decision not to discuss my journey with anyone was further solidified.

It also wasn't hard to keep my secret because at times in my life, I have been truly disappointed in myself. Why couldn't I have lived an even better life? Since I had clearly seen heaven and was so changed by the experience, why did I fail again and again to be the man I truly wanted to be? Why did I fail often to be a reflection of what I had seen and heard and learned?

I guess seeing heaven didn't change the fact that I'm human. Not only human—but also very flawed.

So why share my experience now? Personally, I was perfectly content to keep my silence longer still. But the Lord orchestrated a series of events that convinced me it is now His time to share about my journey to heaven and back. For four decades I *did live* my experience. Now I am compelled to tell how.

In some ways this story is about me. But it is not about me ultimately, nor should it be. It is about God. And it is about you. The two of you together, entwined in a story that, to me, is still breathtakingly sacred. My hope is that you will read not just with your mind but with an open heart. If you do, you may receive more than you bargained for.

My story begins as I pilot a jet on a volunteer missionary flight in the dark of night over Zambia, Africa . . . at 41,000 feet. So please, fasten your seat belt, put your tray table in its upright and locked position, and hold on. It's quite a ride.

For the first time in forty years, here is my story.

—Capt. Dale Black

①
FLIGHT INTO ETERNITY

All passengers and crew will be dead in twenty-seven minutes if something drastic doesn't change.

And I will be responsible.

With very little fuel remaining in our tanks, I'm out of options and out of time. And a lot of things just don't make sense.

The copilot's hand trembles as he brings the microphone close to his ashen face. "Lusaka Approach, Lusaka Tower, Zambia Center. Anyone? Learjet Four-Alpha-Echo. Mayday, Mayday, Mayday."

Still no response.

Thirty-eight-year-old veteran copilot Steve Holmes peers through the jet's windshield from the right seat and demands an answer.

"Where is the city? What is going on here?" He shakes his head slowly in stunned disbelief, for he too has weighed our options, and they are dwindling fast.

Our gleaming luxury jet is equipped with the latest modern avionics package, including dual global navigation systems, but both became INOP (inoperative) over an hour ago. We have no idea why. No one is responding to our radio transmissions either, and in my sixteen years of professional flying, nothing has prepared me for what is happening now.

Nothing could have. I feel my chest constricting as I reach behind me and lock the cockpit door.

Transmitting on one-two-one-point-five, the emergency frequency that all controllers monitor, we try again.

"Mayday, Mayday, Mayday. Learjet November-Four-Two-Four-Alpha-Echo. Can anyone read? Over."

Again nothing. Only the hiss of static.

Trying to slow my breathing and focus my thoughts, I lean forward, looking out the jet's multilayered Plexiglas windshield.

"I've seen campfires from forty thousand feet before, Steve. I don't want to start our descent until we can see the lights of the city. Something should be visible. Keep looking."

Guilt gnaws at my stomach. My heart pounds wildly.

How could I have allowed this to happen? How can so many things go wrong—all at the same time?

As an airline pilot on temporary furlough from Trans World Airlines (TWA), I started a jet pilot training and jet sales corporation in Southern California. I donated airplanes, pilots, and maintenance services to help train and transport individuals to supply Bibles, gospel tracts, medical personnel, and supplies to those in need.

This two-week-long volunteer flight is one of hundreds I've conducted over the last several years, feeling compelled to share God's overwhelming love with others in a hurting world.

This month takes us throughout Europe, the Middle East, and Africa.

So far God has provided the means and the protection to accomplish our mission, but on this flight everything is starting to fall apart. Events are beginning to spiral out of control.

Along with a professional flight planning service, both Steve and I have prepared meticulously for this flight. Three full-time professionals, for three full days, conducted intense flight planning. We accessed the latest international flight data resources and arranged for every foreseeable contingency. We dotted every i and crossed every t—or so we thought.

The latest weather forecast indicated visibility would be unlimited for hundreds of miles around the capital of Zambia, our planned fuel stop. This flight should have been routine even with the extended holding delay required earlier by Sudanese Air Traffic Control.

I pray silently.

Steve rips off his headset and flings it across the cockpit pedestal.

Trying to breathe, trying to steel myself, I speak slowly but firmly. "Steve, we need to work together. Let's believe that God will help us get this aircraft on the ground safely, during our first and only approach. Can you do that?"

Steve shoots me a hard look. "Sure." Then he slams the thick checklist into the Learjet's side pocket. "*Approach Descent Checklist* complete." As a self-proclaimed agnostic, Steve doesn't appreciate my reliance on God. At least not yet.

"I'll land on any runway I can see, Steve. We may be in thin clouds or above a layer of low stratus. The lights of the entire city, the whole country for that matter, may be out for some reason. Now, I've never seen this before, and I've got to admit I've never heard of it either. I know that doesn't explain why we can't see lights from a car, a truck, a campfire, or something. But, Steve, we'll get this aircraft on the ground in just a few minutes, I assure you."

"Flaps 10 degrees," I command.

I hear the familiar whine of flap actuators responding.

Both NAV needles move steadily toward the center of my HSI (horizontal situation indicator), verifying that we are on course. But to where? *Lusaka, right?*

Yes, Lusaka, our planned destination. It must be Lusaka, I tell myself.

"*Glide slope* alive," I continue. "Give me gear down, flaps 20, and the *Before Landing Checklist*."

"Roger, gear coming down, flaps 20, and the Before Landing Checklist."

Seconds later.

"Flaps 40, please."

I hear the tremor in Steve's voice. "Flaps 40 selected, 40 indicated, the Before Landing Checklist is complete."

The sleek jet is all set for landing. No switches need to be moved again until safely on the ground—if we can find a runway. Making minor adjustments on the power levers and flight controls, I keep the speed at precisely 127 knots while adjusting heading and pitch to stay on course and on glide slope. I fly using reference to the instruments only, while Steve peers into the blackness, straining for any sign of an airport and cross-checking my every move.

The muscles in Steve's face visibly tighten as he speaks.

"One thousand feet above *minimums*." *Minimums* means two hundred feet above the runway and the lowest altitude we can safely fly on instruments. Unless we can see a visible runway, we cannot descend below minimums . . . period.

With a feather-like touch on the power levers, I reduce speed a tad while turning right just one degree to stay on course, on speed, and on glide slope.

We will find this runway, on our first approach, I assure myself.

"Five hundred feet above minimums."

"Do you have visual?" I feel my stomach tighten.

"Negative. No visual. No ground contact. One hundred feet above minimums."

Steve shakes his head slowly.

"Keep looking outside, Steve, but call minimums."

A few seconds pass, then Steve winces and barks, "Minimums, minimums. No contact."

For a split second I tear my eyes away from the cockpit instruments to look outside just above the aircraft's long slender nose. Directly ahead there should be a visible runway—only utter blackness stares back. That's when my heart stops.

On the outside I appear calm and cool, but it's only an act.

Forcing my mind to stay in control, I advance the throttles to *go around* thrust for the *missed approach* and pitch the aircraft up to a 15-degree nose-high attitude. My stomach cringes, knowing that the jet's two engines are now guzzling our limited fuel reserves with the force of two fire hoses. At this altitude and with the high drag, we're burning fuel four times faster than at cruise speed. Fuel, our aircraft's life blood, is being sucked dry.

Fighting to keep my thoughts from running wild, Steve and I review our in-flight scenario. There are no clouds, no fog or weather of any kind, verified by the crescent-moon light reflecting off our jet's shiny wings—all the way down to two hundred feet. With a population of over a million people, the city of Lusaka seems to have disappeared. Not a car or truck light is seen. There are no street lights or campfires. We are about down to fumes remaining in the fuel tanks, and at two hundred feet we see no runway—no airport—not even any trace of the *ground*.

It's not just fear that silently strangles me. It's total disbelief. And I can barely breathe.

The radios continue their silence.

In my sixteen years of flying jets and training pilots, I have never heard of this before. *Are we way off course? If so, how far? Are we flying over water? Are we above some invisible layer of fog? Are the altimeters grossly in error?* Nothing makes sense. My once-starched white-collared shirt is now damp and wilted, and my heart is racing.

In a voice just above a whisper I pray out loud, "Lord, what should I do? You always answer prayer; so God, what should I do now?"

While flying a worthless holding pattern twelve-thousand feet somewhere over Zambia, trying to sort out our in-flight midnight emergency, with only minutes of fuel remaining in the Learjet's tanks, my mind flashes back to another flight . . . the life-changing airplane crash in which I was just a passenger—yet the only survivor.

The flight that changed how I see things.

The flight that changed me forever.

The single flight that has defined my very existence.

FRIDAY, JULY 18, 1969

I was nineteen.

It was before daybreak in my hometown of Los Alamitos, about half past four, and the sky was a dove gray with only a light feathering of low clouds. The morning paper had yet to arrive, but the day before, the *LA Times* announced: "Astronauts Prepare Landing Craft as Apollo Nears Moon." The Apollo 11 flight had dominated the news that week. All eyes and ears were on the heavens, tracking the spacecraft's every move, listening to its every transmission. The world was mesmerized. At the moment, though, most of my part of the world, Southern California, was asleep—oblivious to Apollo 11 speeding through space and oblivious to my MGB speeding through its streets on the way to Burbank Airport.[1] A lightweight dark green roadster, it could do 0 to 60 in just over eleven seconds.

What can I say? I was nineteen, with testosterone racing through my veins.

I was an athlete, playing shortstop for Pasadena College, and an aviator on my way to flying jets. I was a driven person, particularly at that time in my life. I went to school full time, played baseball, and worked at my family's business, which manufactured redwood shavings, hauling truckloads off to various places in California for use in landscaping everything from freeways to golf courses. Since childhood I worked in the trucking division, loading and unloading trucks, and performing routine maintenance on the big rigs. Several times a week I came to the plant after hours, looking for some additional work. I often spent my evenings catching up on truck maintenance. Sometimes I would run the packaging machine or baler all

---

[1] Hollywood-Burbank Airport (BUR), mentioned repeatedly in this book, changed its name in 2003 to Bob Hope Airport.

night to fill an order for the next day. But most of the time I would drive an 18-wheeler all night long, filled with bulk redwood shavings, and usually returned just in time to make my morning classes. After paying my way through college, any time and money I had left I spent taking flying lessons at Brackett Air Service in La Verne.

Looking back, I don't know how I did it. The "why" was easy. I wanted everything life had to offer. That meant logging a lot of hours in the classroom, on the playing field, and in the air. All of which took money. I wasn't a trust-fund kid. I didn't get an allowance. I didn't get any help with school, let alone my extracurricular activities. Flying was expensive. Cars were expensive. School was expensive. And though my parents didn't help financially, they did give me the opportunity to work as many hours as I wanted so I could earn the money to pay for those things.

One of those things was the British-made convertible I was driving into the sunrise of a beautiful Southern California morning. Two days of Santa Ana winds had cleared the haze from the San Fernando Valley. The only color in the sky was a streak of orange. The only sound the rpms in my four-cylinder engine, whining for me to shift.

Did I mention I was nineteen?

And did I also mention that a month earlier the college had expelled me? It wasn't a slap-on-the-wrist suspension. It was permanent.

But it didn't matter. With my hand on the gearshift and my pilot's license in my hip pocket, I was living my dream, the star of my own movie.

My life was an action-adventure film waiting for the opening credits to finish so the story could get started and the adrenaline kick in. I was so close to getting that story started. For me, the opening credits were courses taken in school and hours logged in flight.

I shaved a curb with the tires screeching.

Even with Vietnam breathing down my neck, I didn't give a thought to losing my student deferment. After all, I was nineteen, and I was invincible. There were other colleges. And I reasoned that if I didn't get a baseball scholarship to one of them, I'd get one playing football. Other than flying, nothing made me feel more alive than a hard-hitting game of tackle.

But none of that mattered. Not now.

All that mattered was my date with a sleek twin-engine Piper Navajo. Soon I would be in the air, soaring above the snarl of L.A. traffic. All my cares would be behind me, including college with its classwork and course schedules and the thankless, never-ending work of driving a truck.

Once at the airport, I downshifted, careful not to ruffle anyone's feathers. Careful to show proper respect. For this was sacred ground to me, this place where my dreams were on the tarmac, waiting for me to climb into the cockpit and strap on the seat belt.

Ever since I was fourteen, I wanted to become a commercial pilot—to travel, see the world, wear the uniform, live the adventure.

I wanted it all.

And I wanted it bad.

To get there, I needed a mentor. I was meeting with him that morning. His name was Chuck Burns, a twenty-seven-year-old commercial pilot. He had the license, the uniform, the skill, everything. And he was willing to take me under his wing.

I would show up two or three times a week to help him with his work, flying throughout the state to deliver bank checks. Even though I got paid nothing for my efforts, I got to log a lot of flight time. As a young pilot, that was compensation enough, plus it was a golden opportunity to fly in a quality aircraft and learn from an awesome instructor.

I still have the logbook of those early flights. My first flight with Chuck was May 29, 1969, in a Piper Aztec. We had become fast friends. More than friends. He had become like an older brother to me.

I was first to arrive on the tarmac where the red-and-white Piper Navajo was parked. The Navajo was a family of twin-engine planes designed in the mid-'60s by Piper Aircraft and targeted for small-scale cargo operations and the corporate market. The Turbo Navajo could hold up to seven passengers, plus crew, and came with powerful Lycoming engines rated at 310 horsepower each. The propellers were controllable pitch, fully feathering Hartzells. Empty, the plane weighed a little under four thousand pounds with a maximum takeoff weight of almost seven thousand. The maximum speed was 261 mph with a cruising speed of 238.

Chuck and I had taken the Navajo out on the town just the night before. He and I had double-dated, impressing the girls with the lights that were spread over Southern California like a glittering array of jewels on a black velvet background. It had been a beautiful evening—no wind, no clouds, and just a little haze. Chuck had taken off and landed, letting me do the flying in between. We had veered the plane over Van Nuys, then over Los Angeles. Back then, there was limited air traffic control. The air space above three thousand feet was more or less free to roam. And roam we did. Hollywood. Santa Monica. Arcadia. Pasadena. We had seen it all. And, more important, we had impressed our dates. We had gotten home fairly late, so it was an early morning for both of us.

The airplane had flown effortlessly, not giving a bit of trouble or raising any concerns. Even though it had been less than eight hours since our evening flight, I couldn't wait to get back into the air.

It was a thrill to be alone with such an aircraft, its sturdy workhorse function bred with a sleek racehorse form, as beautiful as it was powerful. I checked out the aircraft's structure, examining everything from the wheels to the windshield. I felt like a jockey checking out the Thoroughbred he was about to race, examining the legs, the saddle, the reins.

Everything checked out. That's when I climbed into the cockpit. Sat there a minute, just taking it all in. The dials, the switches. The smell of leather and metal. The feel of my hands gripping the controls. The feel of my dreams ready to take flight.

I made a few checks, then started the engines. They coughed to life but quickly evened out to a strum. The propellers burst into a whirl, then a blur.

The sensation of that much power in your hands, it was exhilarating.

I cut the engines, and all that power died at the touch of a hand. *My hand.*

It was more than exhilarating; it was intoxicating.

I got out of the plane and waited near the aircraft's tail, looking over at the giant commercial jets lined up at their respective gates; over at others taxiing on the tarmac, waiting their turn to take off. My blood stirred as the roar of their massive engines launched them into the air.

Though I grew up in the '60s, I was never a child of the '60s. The whole drug scene passed me by without giving me a second look. I did love a lot of the music, though. Many of the lyrics spoke of drug use. "Eight Miles High" by the Byrds, for example: "Eight miles high, and when I touch down . . ."

These jets could fly eight miles high, literally. I had flown pretty high myself in smaller planes. I was sure that no drug could come close to the feeling of flying that high, especially in that powerful of a plane.

Which made you feel powerful yourself.

You can't imagine the feeling of taking off in one of those things, flying in one, landing one—the final approach . . . the stripes on the runway coming at you at over 100 mph . . . the yelp of rubber as you touch down . . . the roar of the engines catching up to you.

What a rush!

My parents didn't share my enthusiasm for flying. They weren't any different from other parents raising kids in the '60s. There were plenty of things to worry about on the ground—drugs, sex, the British invasion and the music they brought with them, Vietnam. What parent would want to add to the list by putting their kid in an oblong box of metal and letting him take it to forty thousand feet?

And besides, they had hopes that I would stay in the family business. Grandpa, who started it, was there. My dad, who started his own company within Grandpa's business, was there. My two uncles. Mom. Grandma. My brothers and several cousins. It was just kind of expected that I would follow suit.

I think they thought I would get flying out of my system someday and come down to earth, get my feet on the ground, and put my nameplate on a desk in the company office. But they saw how passionate I was about flying—how driven—and they indulged me.

Another jet took off, its surging engines causing something to resonate within me that I can't explain. It was like hearing the most stirring music being played, everything within you reverberating to the music, and in one swelling crescendo speaking to your soul, saying, "This is what you were made for."

My daydreams were interrupted by a pleasant man in his thirties who approached me, offering his hand.

"I'm Gene Bain. I'll be flying with you today."

His handshake was firm and confident.

Gene was a Fresno police officer and a friend of the company's chief pilot. He also had his commercial license and on occasion had flown the route by himself. He also had a good reputation as a pilot, which was important. After all, I was putting my life in his hands.

"Have you gone through a pre-flight and engine run-up yet?"

"Well, not really," I said.

Actually I had, and everything checked out, but I didn't want him to know. I felt too inexperienced to shoulder that much responsibility.

"I did warm up the engines," I confessed, "and conducted the pre-flight on the exterior, but you had better go ahead and check it out yourself."

We'll be twice as safe today, I thought.

A few minutes later Chuck joined Gene and me, and the three of us walked briskly to the plane that was to take us northward to Santa Maria, Coalinga, Fresno, Visalia, Bakersfield, and several other stops in the state.

We climbed aboard and settled into our flight positions. Gene took the pilot's seat. I took the seat next to him, the copilot's seat. And Chuck, the most experienced of us, sat on a temporary third seat behind us so that he could monitor our every move.

The weather was calm. The sky clear. And I felt relaxed as Gene started the engines. The propellers kicked in. So did my heart. Revving in anticipation of taking flight.

As Gene taxied the aircraft toward the runway, though, the calm was broken. He seemed overly abrupt and aggressive on the flight controls. I wondered what his problem was.

Chuck wondered too, though he didn't say anything. He just tapped me on the shoulder and motioned for me to change places with him.

As Chuck fastened his seat belt, we approached Runway 15. We would be making an "intersection departure," our usual procedure. This simply meant that instead of taxiing to the far end of the runway, we would leave from the terminal parking lot where the plane was, and we would take off from the place that intersected with the runway. This meant we would not use the twelve hundred feet of runway that was behind us. By doing that, we saved a little time and a little fuel.

We paused for the necessary engine run-ups and to go through the Before Takeoff Checklist. Gene flipped the switches, checked the gauges. I watched him go through every procedure, procedures that by now I could do with my eyes closed.

All primary and secondary systems checked out.

Chuck watched it all, monitored it all. If he was feeling uneasy, he didn't show it.

At last we were cleared for takeoff. Gene throttled the engines and steered the plane toward the southeast horizon.

Through the window I caught a glimpse of a PSA Boeing 727 taxiing a few hundred feet away. Don't get me wrong, the Navajo was a great plane. But it was dwarfed by the 727. *I will be flying one of those someday,* I thought, which was less of a thought and more of a vow.

Words crackled from the control tower.

"Navajo Five-Zero-Yankee, this is Burbank Tower. You're cleared for takeoff, Runway one-five. After takeoff, turn right, heading two-four-zero, climb and maintain three thousand. Departure control will be on one-two-four-point-six-five."

Chuck spoke into the microphone. "Roger. Navajo Five-Zero-Yankee cleared to go. Runway one-five, right heading two-four-zero, climb and maintain three thousand and twenty-four-sixty-five."

All systems were go. Gene throttled to maximum takeoff power, and the plane accelerated down the runway, causing it to bounce slightly. But that usually happened.

What didn't usually happen was that we were suddenly airborne at an abnormally slow speed. I scanned the dials as questions raced through my mind. *Why were we airborne so soon? Why would Gene take off at less than normal airspeed with the plane fully loaded with fuel and cargo?*

I said nothing. After all, he was a good pilot, I was told, and twice my age.

The engines strained under the weight and the lack of lift. They seemed out of sync with each other. Disturbingly so. Instead of the familiar harmony between the two engines, their rpms gave a dissonant whine.

Something was terribly wrong. I knew it. Chuck knew it. Gene knew it.

Chuck barked the bone-chilling words that confirmed my worst fears. "Let's land in that clear area over there." He pointed toward a cemetery a few hundred yards away.

I held my breath as the sight of pine trees filled the front windshield. *We're not climbing,* I said to myself. *We're not going to clear those trees.*

Every muscle in my body froze.

My God, we're going to crash!

Chuck lunged for the flight controls.

I braced myself for impact.

I was nineteen.

②
PORTAL OF THE FOLDED WINGS

Because of that crash, a part of me would forever be nineteen.

And no part of me would ever be the same.

The last thing I remembered was the sight of Chuck's hands on the controls, violently wrenching the flight controls fully left and fully back.

I remembered nothing of the plane clipping the treetops at eighty feet. I remembered nothing of the plane careening head-on into a seventy-five-foot structure with a mosaic dome. Nothing of the sound of metal slamming into concrete or the plane shattering to pieces. I remembered nothing of the impact with the ground, nothing of the excruciating pain, nothing of the eerie silence that undoubtedly followed and the suffocating smell of airplane fuel that would have hung in the air like a toxic cloud.

What I do remember came back to me in the most fragmentary of ways. A piece at a time. My memory was like a jigsaw puzzle with only a few recognizable pieces and no overall picture to serve as a reference. Besides the pieces that were missing, the pieces I did have were turned over in my mind, without color or clue as to where they fit.

Although I remembered nothing of the fall, for example, for years after the crash I would be jolted awake from a sound sleep by my arms flailing in circles, trying to balance myself as I fell helplessly through the air. That is how things came back to me. A frightful image from a dream. A sudden flash of memory. A newspaper article piecing together the events. An eyewitness handing me some missing piece to the puzzle.

Not only was the plane shattered, pieces of the wreckage lying everywhere, my mind was shattered, twisted pieces of memory scattered over the landscape of the year that stretched before me. Some of what follows was told to me by ambulance personnel, doctors, and friends who visited the crash sight.

Gene and Chuck were thrown from the plane. Gene was not moving. Chuck was lying on the ground, moaning. Apparently I was still in what remained of the cockpit, lying like a rag doll, limp and motionless. The three of us hit the ground within five feet of each other.

I'm not sure how long I lay there. I was later told that the Burbank Tower had summoned an ambulance that arrived eleven minutes after the crash. When paramedics arrived, they found me staggering through the rubble in a state of shock. I was drenched in fuel, both hands clutching my blood-streaked face with parts of the airplane sticking out of my head and legs. They ran to me and gingerly laid me on the ground.

Chuck and I were put into the same ambulance that sped through the streets, siren blaring. When the ambulance arrived at nearby St. Joseph Hospital, a trauma team was scrubbed and ready for us.

At this point, I didn't know where I was or how I got there.

That is what blunt-force trauma does. The brain goes into autopilot mode. It runs the way it was programmed to run without interference from the conscious mind. It takes control, marshaling the body's resources to deal with the trauma the body is experiencing.

As we burst through the doors of the ER, something inexplicable happened, sending me into uncharted territory.

Suddenly I found myself suspended in midair, hovering over the wreckage of my body. My gray pants and short-sleeve shirt were torn to shreds and soaked in blood and fuel.

I had a bird's-eye view of the entire ER and watched the flurry of activity like a bystander. They wheeled the blue gurney I was on into a room about thirty-five-feet square.

They undid the red straps that held me and moved me onto a metal table. I hovered above the end of the table, near my feet, and just below the acoustical tile ceiling.

A thick-boned, gray-headed doctor approached my body, standing near my left shoulder, and began inspecting me. He gently turned my head to the left, focusing on the damage to my face. He went about his work professionally and unemotionally.

What happened to me? I wondered. *Where am I?*

Three nurses were in the room, the shortest of which stood to the doctor's left. The other two were on the opposite side of the table, cutting off what remained of my clothes, working furiously.

It was then I noticed that my hearing was impaired. I was only a few feet away, but I could barely hear any sounds, barely make out any words, though I could see everything clearly and distinctly.

As the trauma team worked feverishly, I felt surprisingly detached. I recognized myself on the table, but felt no anxiety, no sense of urgency, no pain, no sadness, nothing.

It was a schizophrenic feeling, being two places at once, your body on the table below, another very real part of you floating near the ceiling above. *That may be my body,* I thought, *but I'm up here. I can't be dead because I feel so alive.* Amazingly, I wasn't shocked by all this, just curious, still wondering what had happened.

I looked around the room, surveying the surroundings. The floor was covered in white tiles. Within each were tiny bits of black running in one direction. My eyes followed the tiles from the floor, up the wall, where they stopped about shoulder high.

I noticed the medical equipment, the trays with instruments spread out, the medical staff in gowns. It was all cold and sterile.

All the while, I couldn't stop wondering, *This must be a hospital, but why am I here? What happened?*

Then I experienced the first emotions in my suspended state. A commotion was going on to my left in a room partitioned off by gray curtains. I strained to see what was happening, but I couldn't see through the curtains and I wasn't high enough to look over them. The sounds were garbled, and I couldn't make out what was being said, though I sensed urgency.

I was keenly aware of the atmosphere. Intense, filled with anxiety. Suddenly a wave of sadness washed over me. Medical personnel scurried in and out the room. The sense of loss and grief was heavy beyond belief. The worst feeling I've had in my entire life. The ache was so deep and so intense I couldn't think about anything else.

Then suddenly, without warning, a clear and powerful memory flashed into my mind. I was in the fifth grade. I was a tenderhearted kid who had just received Jesus Christ as his personal Lord and Savior. I remember how truly I believed the Bible's teaching about Jesus being God's only Son and that He loved me. I recall how genuinely sorry I was for my sins and how I prayed that night at church camp for Jesus to be my Savior and friend. I was so full of love for Him, full of zeal. Even at that young age I was filled with purpose and peace.

On the heels of that flashback came a new realization. I was no longer that tenderhearted kid. I was selfish and arrogant. A person who loved a lot of things but not the things God loved. A person who had zeal for a lot of things but not for the things the Lord had zeal for.

It was about me. It was all about me. *My* life. *My* career. *My* hopes. *My* dreams.

My rush.

I felt shame, sadness, grief.

The feelings were palpable. They had weight. And I felt like the weight of those feelings was pulling me down.

Then in a heartbeat the heaviness left. I felt light again. Like I was a hot-air balloon that had been untethered from its moorings and was drifting skyward.

I began moving higher, slowly but steadily. I noticed details in the light fixtures as I approached them. I saw into the air-conditioning ducts in the ceiling. I was moving away from my body, slowly . . . out of the room . . . down the hallway.

I began picking up speed. The movement was effortless, and I had no sensation of self-movement. I didn't know where I was going, but I was distinctly aware that some irresistible force was drawing me there.

The speed of my movement increased. I couldn't stop it, couldn't steer it.

I moved faster, faster, and faster still.

Then suddenly . . .

I was gone.

③

AT THE EDGE OF DEATH

The phone rang at my parents' home in Los Alamitos, interrupting my mother's quiet morning routine.

"Mrs. Black?" said the voice on the other end of the phone.

"Yes."

"This is St. Joseph Hospital in Burbank. I'm sorry to tell you this, but ... there's been a plane crash. One man was killed. At this time there are two survivors. Both are in critical condition. One of them is your son."

My mother listened in stunned silence, said she would be right there, and hung up. She dialed my father's office, and the secretary pulled him out of a meeting to tell him the news and that his wife was on the way to pick him up.

Somehow Mom made the drive to Long Beach Shavings Company, where my dad was co-owner. Along the way her thoughts hounded her. *This can't be happening. I should have asked more questions. Why didn't I ask more questions?*

It was as if she had stepped into a nightmare she couldn't wake up from, and her thoughts were terrifying creatures that just kept coming and coming and coming. She couldn't run from them, and she couldn't hide.

She fumbled with the knob on the car radio, hoping to find a newsbreak that might give her more information. Information she desperately wanted to hear and at the same time didn't.

He's alive, she said to herself. *Thank God, he's still alive.* She gripped the steering wheel tighter, more determined, and stomped on the accelerator, not a minute to lose.

Screeching into the company parking lot, Mom ran toward the door where Dad was pacing. She collapsed in his arms, releasing the tears she could no longer hold back.

But this was no time for tears. They had to hurry. Dad rushed her to the car, took the wheel, and raced north on the Long Beach Freeway. They were weaving in and out of traffic, ignoring the blare of horns. Once again Mom turned on the radio, and once again came the news. Both strained to hear over the noise of the traffic.

"A second fatality has been reported in this morning's airplane crash just outside of Hollywood-Burbank Airport. Names are being withheld pending notification of next of kin."

One was still alive! Which one? The rest of the way neither of them spoke, fearing the worst but praying for the best. The trip seemed like an eternity. Finally they slammed on the brakes in the hospital parking lot. They shot out of the car, raced toward the emergency room, and burst through the doors, their faces wringing with emotion.

"*My son.* He was in a plane crash. Is he alive?" my dad asked breathlessly.

Everything in the ER stopped, all eyes riveted on them. The nurse at the desk froze.

"Well, is he alive or not?" my father demanded.

"It depends on what your last name is," she said.

"Black. My son's name is *Dale* Black."

"Yes, sir, your son is alive." Mom almost collapsed. "But let me warn you," the nurse said, "his injuries are massive. He's suffered a tremendous trauma and is in critical condition."

"Can we see him?"

The nurse shook her head. "He's in surgery. You can go to the waiting room and check in. Someone will come out and let you know how he is doing."

Hours passed, painfully uncertain moments at a time. My parents made a few phone calls, and soon the waiting room was full of friends and family, all in a state of shock, some crying, most of them praying. Talking amongst themselves to bolster their courage. Preparing themselves each time someone in hospital scrubs came to update them on my condition.

I was in the operating room for ten hours. Nurses sponged my body of blood and aviation fuel. They hooked me up to various monitors and IVs, put a tube down my throat, and went to work. A tag team of surgeons, nurses, and anesthesiologists labored to keep me alive.

The free fall undoubtedly caused major trauma to my internal organs. There was concern that they had burst, shut down, or suffered severe lacerations. Another concern was for whatever fractures my skeletal structure had sustained. The primary area of focus, though, was the neurological system. Was there brain damage? Spinal cord injury?

A husky-looking doctor came into the waiting room. "The Black family?" he called. Every conversation stopped. Mom and Dad made themselves known.

"We're his parents."

"Dr. Graham."

Dr. Homer Graham was one of the best orthopedic surgeons in the country. I was in the best care possible. But my parents didn't know this at the time. All they knew was what they'd gotten from the radio on the way to the hospital and then what they heard from the nurse at the front desk.

"He's alive."

"Oh, thank God," they said, breathing a sigh of relief.

"We're still working on him. Should be a long day. Things are touch and go. But we've got a good team in place, and we'll give him our best."

It was indeed a long day, both for the people in the operating room and for the ones in the waiting room. At the end of the day, Dr. Graham came out again, his gown drenched with sweat.

"How is he?" my dad asked.

"Both ankles and knees were broken. Both legs fractured. His back was broken in three places."

My mother gasped. "Is he—"

"Paralyzed?" the doctor said. "Too early to tell."

The doctor paused, seeing these were painful words for my parents. Then he continued.

"His left arm and shoulder were severely damaged. The ball-and-socket in his left shoulder exploded on impact. His right arm was fractured. His left ankle was crushed beyond repair."

My mother bit back the tears, wondering about the ramifications of "beyond repair."

"Debris from the aircraft penetrated both legs. His face was brutally lacerated with a gash through the middle of his forehead, eyebrow, and into his right eye," the doctor said, indicating on his own face where the gash occurred. "The right side of his head was virtually shaved off. We'll do the best plastic surgery we can . . ." He paused, searching for the right words. "Regardless, he won't look the way he used to."

The avalanche of bad news buried my parents. All they could do was stand there, frozen and numb.

At last my father spoke. "What's the prognosis, long term?"

"If he survives, he won't regain use of his left arm and leg. All the doctors concur. Paralysis is a threat; we'll be watching closely for that. He'll be blind or nearly blind in his right eye. And—" he paused— "there's a strong possibility of brain damage. He survived a strong blow to the head; it's reasonable to assume he didn't survive it without some permanent damage. The next twenty-four to forty-eight hours are critical."

The words *if he survives* resounded in my parents' thoughts over the days ahead, echoing in the empty moments when they were alone. Walking the hallways of every waking hour. Haunting the stillness at night. Staring at them in the morning.

If he survives . . .

4

NEW EYES FOR A NEW DIMENSION

For three days I was in a coma. I was watched around the clock, nurses shuffling in and out at all times of the day and night to check my vitals, change my bandages, see if the stitches were holding, if the swelling was under control.

My parents were at the hospital much of the time. My grandparents came, my brothers, my aunts and uncles. Friends from school. Co-workers at the company. They prayed, they cried, they worried, and they wondered. *Would I survive? Would I be paralyzed? Would I be brain damaged? Would I walk again? Talk again? Play sports again?*

After three very difficult days, of which I had no memory, I regained consciousness. It was early morning of the fourth day, Monday, July 21.

I awoke slowly, groggily, with a strange sensation in my head. It was the sound of glorious music dying away, as if I had just heard the last note of a crescendo that was resonating in the air after it had been played. Now other sounds pushed themselves into the foreground—the sound of rubber-soled shoes scurrying dutifully about in the hallway, of people's voices muffled outside my door, of wheels rolling over linoleum.

I tried to remember where I was. I had a dim memory that it was a hospital, but no memory of what had put me there. Pain smoldered throughout my body, although the drugs kept it from flaring up and raging out of control. It also kept me from thinking straight. *What happened? How did I get here?*

A nurse in a pair of those rubber-soled shoes, with one of those muffled voices, quietly stepped onto the linoleum that led to my bed, careful not to disturb me. She smiled while she checked the IVs. I tried to speak, but my voice was garbled. And when I did speak, I felt this tearing sensation as if my face were being ripped open.

The nurse looked at me, studying the reactions in my good eye. "Hello, Dale," she said. "How do you feel? Can you hear me?"

This is hard to explain, but I felt an immediate and overwhelming love for this woman. It wasn't romantic. Nothing like that. It was deeper than that, purer. I wanted to talk with her, to thank her for helping me, but I couldn't. Most of all, I wanted to encourage her by telling her just how much God loved her.

Much of my face and all of my head were covered in bandages. I had stitches in my right eye, and the lid itself had been stitched shut. I could see clearly out of my left eye, but something was different.

The first words I remember saying were "What happened to my eyes?" I wasn't referring to the stitches or the bandages. Even though only one eye was working, it seemed as if I was looking out of both of them. I was seeing with what seemed to be two perfectly healthy eyes. But they were not only healthy, they were strengthened somehow. Nothing looked the same.

It felt as if I were seeing a new dimension, like 4-D, another level of reality. It was as if I had seen the world through a filter all my life, like a film had been over my eyes all these years and now that film was removed. In a very real sense, I was seeing with new and strengthened eyes.

That's how I was seeing this nurse. I had never met her, didn't even know her name. It was not a human love, I was sure of that. It was God's love. I felt as if I were a vessel through which His love was flowing. *Does she know Jesus?* was the first thought that came to my mind. I had met a lot of women in college, and I wondered a lot of things about them. I thought the same things any nineteen-year-old boy would think. Thoughts about appearance. Thoughts about personality. Thoughts about sense of humor.

But thoughts about Jesus Christ, the Son of God, and whether they knew Him? It wasn't even on my radar screen.

The next thoughts were *What if she has an accident and dies? What then? Will she go to heaven?*

I couldn't remember ever having thoughts like this about people. It was strange. Again, it was like seeing in a new dimension. Like watching a 3-D movie with unaided eyes, then suddenly putting on the 3-D glasses. Something indeed had happened to my eyes. And it was infinitely deeper than the gash. If anything, the gash I experienced was severing the veil that separated the physical dimension from the spiritual.

When she left the room, I reflected on the encounter. *What is happening to me? Why am I . . .* But before I could think anything else, the drugs lulled me back to sleep.

I woke to a doctor standing beside my bed. "Good morning, Dale. I'm Dr. Graham. How are you doing today?"

The same feeling came over me. I felt enormous love for this stranger standing beside me. *Why?* I wondered. I had never met him before. Didn't know anything about him, except what he just told me.

"You've been in an accident, Dale," the doctor explained. "A plane crash. You just rest. We'll take good care of you. You've had some serious injuries, but you're going to be OK. You may have trouble remembering things . . . you've had a severe head injury . . . just rest now."

I felt as if I knew this man. *But how? How could that be?* And yet . . . his demeanor . . . his hair . . . his hands . . . his voice. I had seen him before, heard him before. I didn't know how I knew him, but I did. I felt it deeply and with great conviction.

I watched the doctor scribble notes on my chart. As he did, I felt such tenderness toward him. It seemed as if our roles had been reversed. I was looking at him with feelings a doctor would normally have for his patient. It was weird, something I had never experienced before. How do you explain love for someone you've never met? Not sympathy. Not only compassion. But love. A deep and inexplicable love.

It was beyond me, I knew that.

It was beyond human, I knew that too.

I couldn't remember the crash Dr. Graham had mentioned. I couldn't remember anything. It was as if my mind had been taken away and a heart put in its place. A new heart. A real heart. A working heart. The way hearts were meant to work.

I no longer saw the uniform a person wore, let alone desired the uniform for myself, the position for myself, the prestige for myself, the pay for myself. Somehow—don't ask me how—I saw the person's heart and felt enormous love and compassion. I wanted to know each person who crossed my path, from the doctors to the orderlies. I wanted to know their stories, their heartaches. I felt compassion for complete strangers, which was so unlike the person I was before.

It was strange. No, it was supernatural. I don't know what happened during those three days in a coma, but something happened that I couldn't explain. A new way of seeing. Which was leading me to a new way of thinking and feeling. And ultimately to a new way of living.

Is it the morphine? I wondered. *Is it the trauma of the crash that is working its way mysteriously through my psyche?*

I didn't know. I feared it might go away as my body healed. Only time would tell if the change was real . . . and if it was permanent.

As the morphine wore off and I began to be weaned from stronger to weaker painkillers, my new sight remained intact, and my new love for people only increased.

There had been a Copernican shift in my thinking. Before the crash, I was the center of my solar system. Everything orbited around me and for me. Now I was a lesser planet that orbited around something bigger than myself. And that something bigger was the one true God.

Somehow I had been given *His* heart for people. *Any* people. *All* people. Friends. Family. Co-workers. Complete strangers.

Maybe the shift wasn't so much in my thinking as it was in my feeling. Not so much in my head as in my heart. Because it wasn't an intellectual discussion I was having with myself. Or a theological one. It was personal. Deeply, profoundly, and unalterably personal.

No, it wasn't the morphine.

The feelings were real, and they were permanent.

With the decrease in drugs, there was an increase in pain. I felt like a burnt marshmallow, all puffy and hot. The chemicals in the fuel had burned my skin, and it was reddening, swelling, and peeling off.

I tried moving, but it was terribly uncomfortable and painful. I was in so many casts and bandages I felt like a mummy. Hooked up to so many tubes and wires, I felt tied to my bed. It was claustrophobic. I had no idea what I looked like. If I looked anything like I felt, I was in deep trouble. The staff was very professional. The doctors never flinched when they examined me. The nurses didn't wail like peasant women at the funeral of a child when they changed my bandages. And none of the orderlies gawked as if I were a sideshow at a circus.

Then my brother Darrell came to visit.

He took one look at me, rushed to the bathroom, and threw up. The retching. The heaving. The flushing. I'll never forget it.

And I'll never forget thinking, *Do I look that bad?*

Dr. Graham checked on me several times a day and he never threw up. He did, however, wonder how I had made it this far, looking at me as I lay there—a miracle of modern medicine and at the same time a mess.

He tested my sight by putting a pen in front of my unbandaged eye and having me track it. He touched a bare patch of skin to see if I had feeling, asking what I may have remembered.

Next to nothing.

I did, however, remember my parents. I especially remember the day they came to the hospital dressed in their Sunday clothes. My dad brought me the Bible they had given me when I graduated from high school. I had hardly opened it since then. Now I couldn't wait to read it. It surprised me how eager I was. I held it in my hand like a newfound treasure. After thumbing through it for a while, I put it down, eager to talk about something else that was on my heart.

"How's Chuck?" I asked.

Neither said a word.

"What about Chuck?"

My dad walked to the window, looked outside, and pointed. "He's buried out there. We just got back from the funeral."

"They were both killed," my mom said.

I kept that knowledge outside me, letting only a little in. It was too much. I couldn't bear it. And I couldn't bear breaking down in front of my parents. They told me Chuck had died in the ambulance. I was so stunned I couldn't speak.

"And if you could have seen the remains of the plane, you'd understand what a wonder it is you are alive." Dad's eyes welled up as he spoke. "God clearly spared your life."

How can it be? I thought. *Why did I survive? The kid who just got his pilot's license the month before. The kid with all the visitors, the cards, the gifts, the flowers. The kid basking in all the attention.*

I was the wonder kid, written about in the morning papers, marveled at on the nightly news, creating a stir at the hospital and sympathy in my friends. Chuck and Gene? They were dead.

I don't remember anything my parents said after that. I didn't want to face the pain of it all, the guilt. I didn't want to talk about it, but I knew that was all people wanted to talk about. The crash. And what a miracle it was that I survived.

To me, it felt nothing like a miracle. It felt like a mistake.

I had survived. Not Gene, the pilot that was better than me. Not Chuck, the pilot that was better than both of us.

My remorse for Chuck was more than I could handle. For the first time since I met him, I worried about his eternal destiny. All the time I had spent with him, and I never told him about God's only Son, Jesus. All the destinations we talked about traveling to someday, and I never talked to him about the one destination that mattered. The pain of that was unbearable. The drugs, the visitors, and the distraction of having my bandages changed gave me a brief reprieve But when I was alone, those thoughts came rushing back. And it was everything I could do to keep my head above those incriminating waters.

Why was I having those feelings about Chuck? About the doctor. And the nurse.

What was happening to me?

5

UNDER HIS WINGS

When Dr. Graham came to visit again, I was more lucid. And more curious.

"What happened to Chuck?"

Dr. Graham was like a machine. He showed no emotion, no reaction at all. "He died in the OR. We tried for twenty minutes to resuscitate him."

"What was the cause of death?"

"Blunt trauma," Dr. Graham said matter-of-factly.

"Was he the one in the emergency room . . . behind the curtains?"

Dr. Graham nodded.

So he didn't died in the ambulance as my parents thought.

"The other man was pronounced dead at the scene. He died on impact."

I closed my eye. I felt the breath leave my lungs, the very life in me escaping. That was the end of his visit, the end of my day, a dark and lonely end.

On another visit, on another day, my parents were with the doctor. He was going to give me my prognosis and wanted them there for support.

"When are you going to let me out of here, Doc?"

He looked at my parents, then back to me. "Dale, it looks to us at this time that you'll be hospitalized for at least eight months. You have some pretty severe injuries. You're going to require extensive specialized rehabilitation. And we want to keep a close eye on you for head and other internal injuries."

Whether it was faith, youthful enthusiasm, or some genetically ingrained stubbornness, I can't say, but I felt emboldened and blurted out: "I'll be flying over that monument as pilot in command one year from the day of the crash!"

No one smiled. No one encouraged me. They just stared at me in silence. And then, saying their polite good-byes, they left.

Later, a copy of the *LA Times* from the day after the crash found its way onto my bed. The front-page headlines read: "PLANE CRASHES INTO AIR MEMORIAL. TWO MEN DIE, ONE CRITICAL."

I scanned it with my good eye: "Seconds after taking off from Hollywood-Burbank Airport, a twin-engine plane crashed into a cemetery's memorial to aviators Friday morning, killing two men and critically injuring a third. Dead were the pilot, Charles Burns, 27, of Lakewood, and copilot, Eugene Bain, 38, of Fresno. A passenger, Dale Black, 19, of Los Alamitos was taken to St. Joseph Hospital in Burbank in critical condition."

Beside the article was a photograph of the monument we had hit. The ornate cubical structure with the dome on top was built as a memorial to fallen pioneers of aviation history. And there, at the base of that memorial, was what was left of our plane. Our Piper's mangled wings were lying on the ground, folded one over the other.

Other newspapers found their way into my room, describing the monument and giving details of the crash. The cement and marble memorial was seventy-five feet high and fifty feet by fifty wide. The plane impacted the dome just below the top, at the seventy-foot mark. Judging by the gouge left and the damage to the aircraft, the FAA estimated the speed at impact to be 135 mph. The word used in one of the articles to describe the condition of the aircraft after the crash was *disintegrated*.

On the wall above the wings of our plane was the inscription and name of the monument: PORTAL OF THE FOLDED WINGS.

Aerial photograph taken within hours of the crash. Just visible are shorn-off trees and the impact site on the Portal of the Folded Wings' dome. Photo taken and used with permission by Harold Morby.

A closer view of the crash site, showing a fire truck, emergency personnel, and the Piper Navajo debris. Photo taken and used with permission by Harold Morby.

The plane that had been so vibrant with power, humming life, promise of adventure, was now on the ground like a featherless baby bird fallen from its nest. Frail. Broken. Irretrievably broken.

As I was sifting through the emotional wreckage, picking up the pieces, trying to make some sense of it all, trying to find some peace, two visitors came and tossed what I had gathered to the ground.

The men were pilots, employees of the company that owned the Navajo. They came, ostensibly, to check on me, to see how I was doing. I had trouble remembering them, but they clearly knew me. The conversation quickly turned to a small newspaper that had apparently blamed me for the crash. The reporter, they told me, said that since I was in the temporary seat behind the other two pilots, I was sitting next to the fuel selector valves. And since the plane had lost power after takeoff, they told me my feet probably moved against the valves, closing them, and causing the engines to lose power. The logical blame pointed to me, they said.

I was so taken aback by the accusation that I couldn't respond. I pretended not to understand, pretended to be drowsy from the medication, and they left without my making a rebuttal. In my mind, none of it seemed logical. But my mind wasn't working all that well. What if it was true? What if I *had* been to blame?

No one could have said anything more devastating. I could live without playing sports. I could live without walking. I could live without flying. But *this*? I couldn't live with this.

At the time, I was living with a tremendous amount of physical pain. I could feel the gash across my eyes, feel the stitches in my eyelid, feel the pull of stitches with the slightest movement in my face. My head felt as if it were going to explode. My whole body ached. My back hurt with every breath. My left shoulder throbbed. My left ankle shot skewers of pain up my leg. And I would be that way for the next eight months? The worst was the thought that I was somehow responsible.

If God spared me, was it for this reason? To be summoned before a jury of my peers? Brought before them not to be celebrated but shamed?

A bystander took this photo of his son next to the mangled cockpit. Two years later Dale met the boy and was given the photo.

However severe the physical pain, the emotional pain was worse. Overwhelmed by both, I lay motionless, staring at the ceiling, my mind wandering in a daze amid the wreckage not only of shattered dreams but a shattered faith.

My father's words came back to haunt me: *God clearly spared you.*

From what? Death with dignity?

A war raged between my mind and heart. Had God spared me or sentenced me? Was I sentenced to life without parole, imprisoned by guilt, shame, humiliation, and accusation?

No. A merciful God had not spared me.

A merciful God would have let me die. Wouldn't He?

The visit of those two pilots put me in a bad place. But it was only a place I visited; I didn't dare stay there. In my heart, the deepest part of me, I knew that a loving God had truly spared my life.

Another part of the reason I didn't stay there was the wonderfully cheerful hospital staff. I had become something of a celebrity and they seemed to enjoy it. They seemed to enjoy me too, which made a huge difference in my mood, which went up and down on an almost hourly basis, tracking with my pain and whatever news happened to find its way into my room.

The days that followed brought with them a revolving door of visitors. "You're *worse* than a celebrity, Dale," one of the nurses quipped. "Who *are* all these people, anyway?"

People I knew from high school showed up to see the miracle that survived the unsurvivable. People I knew from the college I had been kicked out of came by to see what had become of me. Lots and lots of people came. It was all a blur.

It seemed that in every conversation I would eventually hear the same words: "You're so lucky to be alive, Dale." I recoiled from the words. It was amazing to have survived what the FAA called a non-survivable airplane crash. But was it really luck? It couldn't be. There was something more to this than luck. God had chosen to spare my life. I knew it was an absolute miracle. Beyond that, I didn't know.

Through the many friends and acquaintances that stopped by, I had a virtual mirror held up to me, reflecting just how bad things were inside my brain.

One day a group from my high school came by, reminiscing about old times. They talked about one of the teachers we'd had. Everyone in the room laughed, bantering back and forth. Everyone but me, that is. I stared at them, bewildered. *Who are they talking about? And who are all the other people they speak of so casually, like I should know them?*

I couldn't even remember most of the people who were visiting. I not only forgot their names, I forgot *them*. I didn't know who they were. They were complete strangers.

And yet to hear them laugh and carry on, you'd think we were best friends. *Are we? Could it be that I have forgotten who my friends are?*

Later, others from college dropped by, and the same thing happened. After everyone left, I stared at the walls, wondering who I was. My eyes drifted to the IV tethered to my arm. The steady drip made me feel like it was happening to my brain. All the memories, all the people I knew, my friends, even my close friends, were steadily dripping out of my mind. *Will I continue to forget? Am I losing my mind?*

I was aware of my surroundings. I wasn't crazy. I was coherent. I could think. I could follow people's conversations, engage in conversation. I just had these gaping holes in my memory.

And by *gaping*, I mean so big you could drive an 18-wheeler through it.

Visitors continued to come by. I had survived. Their prayers had been answered. And now they were there to cheer me on to recovery. I tried to concentrate. I tried to remember their faces, their names, what they meant to me. Then I stopped trying to make sense of all the remember-when stories, all the good-natured kidding, all the comments they thought would lead to conversation. But that led nowhere. I did a lot of smiling and nodding, as if I understood. A lot of grimacing too, hoping they would see the pain I was in, politely excuse themselves, and leave.

My parents sensed my frustration. "Don't worry, Dale, you've had some slight head injuries. It's probably just temporary," they said, trying to console me. But I knew my parents always looked on the bright side.

I *knew* what was going on. I knew I wasn't just suffering from *slight* head injuries. And I was afraid it wasn't temporary.

Even though my injuries were serious, no one told me *how* serious. Their initial assessment was that I had broken a few bones.

Well, I might have only one good eye, but I could see that it was more than just a few broken bones. *What* isn't *broken*? I wondered. *Why isn't anyone telling me the truth?*

I could take the truth. What I couldn't take was the fear of not knowing how bad it was.

My room overlooked the Ventura Freeway, and with my one good eye I watched the cars speed by. I watched and then I wept. I wept for the people inside the cars.

I couldn't understand it, but those people mattered to me. Each and every one of them mattered. Even though I didn't know their names. The type of car they drove didn't matter. My head wasn't turned if it was a Porsche. And it wasn't turned away if it was a Rambler. None of that mattered anymore. It was the person behind the wheel that mattered. Their final destination mattered. Their spiritual destination. And it mattered like nothing else I had ever experienced.

These people need to know about God, I remember thinking. *Not some vague, warm and fuzzy, feel-good concept of God. They need to know the one true God. Those people may think they know where they are going today, but the truth is that most of them are lost. They need to know Jesus Christ, need to know how much He loves them, what He did for them to pave the way to eternity. They can't get there by any road, no matter how smooth it is or how attractive the scenery is along the way. He is the way, the only way. They need Him.*

My thoughts surprised me.

My feelings surprised me even more.

I wept for these people, these people I didn't know who were on their way to somewhere else and in such a hurry to get there.

I stared at the ceiling, dumbfounded. *What has happened to me? I've never thought these thoughts before, never felt these feelings before.* I wasn't the same person I was before the crash. Somehow the answer had to be related to those three days in a coma.

It had to be.

If I could only remember . . . something . . . anything . . .

6

SHRINE TO AVIATION

Because of all the painkillers in my bloodstream, sleep came and went during all hours of the day and night. One day seemed to blend into the next without my being aware of the passage of time.

At some point I began to think about who I was. I didn't focus on all that had happened, things I couldn't remember; I focused on all that *was* happening. To me. Everything about me seemed different. Physically, mentally, emotionally, spiritually.

I felt like the six-million-dollar man. Remember the TV show? He had been in some kind of tragic accident, and the military completely rebuilt him. That's *exactly* what I felt like. Parts of me were definitely me. But parts of me definitely weren't. Who was this new Dale Black?

I thought it was time to take a look.

There was a mirror inside the tray next to my bed. I hadn't bothered to use it before; now I felt compelled to. I pulled the cord to call the nurse. She moved the tray over my bed and lifted the mirror for me.

The startled expressions on some of the faces of visitors seeing me for the first time somewhat prepared me. But nothing could have prepared me for the monster in the mirror.

My hair had been completely shaved off. My head was red and purple, swollen, and bandaged. A crooked railroad line of stitches ran across my forehead and below the bandage over my right eye. One especially nasty gash ran roughshod across my face and chin, held together with gnarly-looking stitches. My nose had been broken and was flat, as if it had been mashed down by some irrepressible force. And burns from the airplane fuel had swollen my skin, discoloring it and distorting it hideously.

This was no six-million-dollar man staring back at me. This was Frankenstein's monster—the work of a mad scientist—an utterly grotesque assemblage of parts, held together by wires and screws, stitches and bandages, rods and plaster casts.

I didn't even look human. I certainly bore no resemblance to the young man with a bright future ahead of him who had boarded that ill-fated plane. The injuries were so severe, the burns so pervasive, the gashes so deep, that all hope for a somewhat normal appearance left me. This was not the kind of thing that cleared up in a few months of bed rest. This was horrifying. This was permanent. This was me.

Now I knew why my brother had thrown up.

I was surprised more people hadn't.

Body building, one of my favorite pastimes, was definitely out. I couldn't even lift my arms. And what about baseball and football? It would be a real surprise if I ever walked again. Forget about diving to catch a pass or going after a hard-hit ground ball. It was over.

I was forever being examined, X-rayed, probed, and injected. An entourage of doctors came through, discussing my case among themselves, asking each other questions and talking about me in the third person as if I weren't in the room.

Results from the tests trickled in, but none of them trickled down to me. I was left in the dark. No one told me the extent of my injuries or the prognosis for my recovery.

Then, finally, after a week of tests, Dr. Graham came to my room and talked to me about the results. "When you first arrived in the hospital after the accident," he said, "we assumed your internal injuries to be severe. And we were particularly concerned about your head injuries and potential brain damage."

As I mentioned before, Dr. Graham was a renowned orthopedic surgeon. I learned from the hospital staff that he was known as the doctor of the stars, having treated a number of celebrities. His best-known patient was Evel Knievel, whose fame was built around daredevil stunts with his motorcycle—everything from jumping over a world's record number of cars to jumping over the Snake River Canyon.

Dr. Graham continued: "I'm aware of the fact that you're still experiencing memory loss, but everything else with regard to your brain looks pretty good. Though we don't understand why, we see no indication of internal injuries. Most of your injuries are related to bone, ligament, and muscle problems. That's *good* news. Anyway, I've talked with your parents and we're going to let you go home tomorrow."

Tomorrow! I thought. *That's a miracle! The original estimate was eight months! And I'm going home in eight days?!* I was stunned.

Later that day my parents and my brother Don arrived. They were overjoyed at the news. And they were fully committed to whatever it took—however long—for me to recover.

"You know, Dale," my dad said, "one big reason this is possible is because your mom has decided to take a leave of absence from the family business so she can take care of you full time."

My brother chimed in with his characteristic sense of wry humor. "And don't worry, Dale, we've hired three drivers to take your place at the plant."

I laughed. And boy did it hurt. My face, my ribs, everything hurt. But a laugh never felt so good.

When I woke up the next morning, my first thought was *I'm getting out of here! I'm going home!*

I could hardly wait. The check-out procedures took forever, but a nurse finally arrived with a wheelchair and painstakingly worked me into it.

As my brother wheeled me down the hallway, I asked my dad, "Would you mind driving by the place where the plane crashed? I'd like to see what it looks like."

Dad was walking to my left; my mom, to the right. Neither said a word.

My brother broke the silence: "Are you sure you can handle that right now? It's only been a little over a week since the crash."

"Yeah. I'd really like to see it for myself." And then I said, trying to reassure them, "I'll be OK."

"Alright, Dale," Dad said with a sigh, "if you're sure."

No sooner were the words out of my mouth than I wondered if I *would* be OK. Wondered what it would be like seeing the grim monolith that was the face of death for Chuck and Gene. Wondered what memories would come back.

Feared what memories would come back.

When we were finally outside the hospital, the warmth of the morning sun was the first thing I felt. It seemed as if I had been in an artificially lit cave for the past eight days, with artificially cooled air mingled with smells of all things sterile. I took a deep breath of fresh air. It brought life . . . and hope.

I was out of the hospital and on my way to recovery. However hard it would be, however long it would take, I was on my way. And it felt great.

As they wheeled me to the car and settled me into the front seat, I took a final look at the hospital. A well of emotions rose to the surface. So much had happened there in just a week. So much death. So much life. So many experiences. So many changes.

We drove north on Hollywood Way from St. Joseph toward Hollywood-Burbank Airport. The cemetery lay just south of it. We turned on a tiny street called Valhalla Drive, which came to an abrupt dead end.

"There's the mausoleum ahead of us, Dale." Dad parked the car along the curb.

I strained with my good eye to focus on the concrete-and-marble domed building that rose seven stories high. It was a drab structure surrounded by a black fence. I don't know what I was expecting, but it wasn't this. I was told we had hit a monument in the center of the cemetery, and I had imagined a large tombstone of some kind or a small mausoleum for a family. I wasn't prepared for anything this size. It was huge. More than huge, it was massive.

None of us got out of the car. None of us spoke. For several minutes we sat in silence, until at last my brother made a comment.

"Except for the engines and the tail, you could have picked up any piece of that airplane with one hand," he explained in a voice barely above a whisper.

Dad raised his arm and pointed. "Your plane sheered off those trees just before impact. Apparently, that's what turned your plane into the monument." He pointed to the crater in the concrete dome, just five feet from the top. "The damage to the air memorial is minor compared to your aircraft. They haven't even finished cleaning up everything yet," he said, indicating the debris on the ground.

What was left of the plane had been removed. I could see gouges in the ground where the plane had dug in. Then I noticed the gilded letters on the side of the memorial:

PORTAL OF THE FOLDED WINGS

The scene spun in my head, and turbulent emotions surged within me, followed by a series of questions: *What is wrong with my memory? Why can't I remember this? How does someone forget something so huge? What really happened barely a week ago?*

Then the big question, the one that loomed over me like some haunting apparition: *Why was I the only survivor?*

I couldn't sort it all out. My mind hurt. It felt as if it were going to explode. I started to panic, and so I took slow, deep breaths to stave off the attack. I hung my head, noticing the grass for the first time. It was dingy and ugly, browned by the scorch of the mid-summer sun. I looked up again. The monument looked old and a little dingy itself, having weathered decades of summer suns.

I couldn't stop looking at the structure, marveling at it, wondering about it. I was drawn to it in ways I couldn't understand, like a curious insect drawn to a glowing bulb.

The irony was impossible not to notice—this memorial to deceased aviators had taken the lives of two more. Inside the structure were plaques to their memory. Outside, where Chuck and Gene had died, there were no plaques.

I had flown over it scores of times. Even that seemed mysterious to me. A sense of destiny came over me as I sat there in the car staring. It was intriguing. At the same time it was indicting. I felt as if it were taunting me somehow. As we sat at the end of Valhalla Drive, everyone had something to say. I was quiet, my mind busy with its own questions, all of which eventually came around to one: *Could it be true that I had caused the crash?*

7

DESTINED FOR THE SKY

It was good to be home. Good to be pampered by my mom instead of the nurses. Not to mention the food. There's nothing like your mother's cooking, especially when you're sick. I ate it up. The food. The pampering. The familiar surroundings. It was wonderful.

I was in a hospital bed, which they had placed in the den. I had lots of time to think, pray, dream. Invariably all my dreams led to one: flying.

I mentioned my dream of becoming an airline pilot began when I was fourteen.

Since the age of twelve, I had been working at my grandfather's business, "the plant," as we called it, and at my father's Long Beach Redwood Corporation, the landscaping products and trucking company next door. I loved working in the family business. I felt like royalty, part of a rich bloodline with the secure destiny of being one of the heirs to the throne, possibly running it all someday along with my brothers.

I had started with the most menial tasks, working my way up through the ranks. There were no special privileges, no fast track to success, despite my pedigree as one of the boss's sons. I swept, I cleaned, I sacked sawdust, I baled shavings. Then I began doing truck maintenance on my dad's 18-wheelers. Small repairs at first and routine maintenance, but gradually I took on more and more responsibility. Later, I logged a million miles driving the big rigs throughout the state delivering the products the business produced.

I also worked hard in order to learn Spanish and could talk with some of the workers, which they appreciated. It bonded us in a special way. It felt like one big hardworking family. And I was a part of it.

There was no job too small for me to do and no job too big that I couldn't someday do it. I felt confident working there. There was a lot of hope in the business. My dad had a can-do attitude. "If you can dream it, you can achieve it," he was fond of saying. Earl Nightingale, the motivational speaker, had been a big influence in his life. Dad had listened to all his tapes. His if-you-think-you-can-you-can philosophy permeated the company. Dad wouldn't allow the word *can't* in our vocabulary. He had always encouraged his workers to bring him their problems, but they had to first write out the problem and have two possible solutions written out with it. "Think it out, then write it out" was another thing you would hear him say. Dad was an outstanding businessman with impeccable integrity.

It's hard to think of a fourteen-year-old as having a philosophy of life, but all those things worked themselves into my thinking and set my course from that time forward.

That same year, something happened that changed who I was and what I wanted to do with my life. My grandfather received an unexpected financial bonus and decided to take the family on a trip around the world. We were in no way a wealthy family, but that summer it felt like we were. We traveled to Berlin and saw the Berlin Wall. We toured the Middle East. We went to Paris. France was so old and so beautiful in contrast to the United States. Paris at night was magical, quite possibly the most beautiful city in the world. And the girls. You can't imagine the effect the French girls had on the pubescent boy I was then. I felt I was becoming a man. And that felt really good. Because of the magnificent lights, the lure of Paris at night was almost addictive. Being there planted seeds within me to want to travel and see the world.

We flew everywhere and saw as much of that world as we could see in a three-week period. Switzerland was my favorite. But there was Austria. Italy. Lebanon. Syria. Egypt. We traipsed through the ruins of an empire in Rome and traveled through the pages of the Bible in Jerusalem. We saw the *Mona Lisa* in the Louvre and the most beautiful women in the world in Italy and Scandinavia.

Everywhere we went, we were treated royally. We were looked up to because we were Americans, and the rest of the world still treasured the memories of our involvement in World War II. England, France, Denmark, Italy, they were all so appreciative, mainly because there were so many people still alive who had fought in that war, who had lost fathers and sons in that war, who had cheered American soldiers as they liberated Europe, city by war-torn city.

Pretty amazing experiences for a kid on the cusp of growing up. The most amazing experience, though, was not any one place we traveled to or any particular sight we saw when we got there. The most amazing things to me were the TWA Boeing 707s we traveled on and the pilots that flew them.

The size of the jet, the sheer power of its engines, the thrill of liftoff, the sound of the landing gear being retracted, the ease at which the massive machine cut through the air, these were all mesmerizing. And then, before you knew it, you were at thirty thousand feet, looking down on fleecy expanses of clouds, and through breaks in the clouds to cities, farmlands, oceans that spread as far as the eye could see, sunlight glinting off their scalloped surfaces.

The pilot behind all this power stood so tall and nonchalant in his crisply pressed uniform as you boarded his plane, smiling, greeting us as if we were someone special. His demeanor was a picture of confidence and control, someone who was trained and could be trusted. Then there was the thrill of hearing his voice over the loudspeaker telling us what we could see out the left window. Or letting us know when we were about to encounter turbulence and not feeling the least bit worried because his voice was so calm and reassuring.

When our travels were over, I was a different person, with new dreams that captivated me, new sights on my horizon, new adventures that stretched ahead of me.

I wanted to be one of those pilots, flying one of those jets to exotic parts of the world. But it seemed out of reach for a teenager who sacked his granddad's wood sawdust and repaired his father's trucks in what now seemed a small and shop-worn part of the world.

Then at that pivotal age of fourteen, something else happened. Someone I had always known, who was an engineer and vice-president of our company, helped me look at my life differently. His name was Ron Davis, one of my dad's best friends, who that year became *my* best friend. My dad was a responsible, hardworking man, intent on building a business to provide for his family and to pass it on to his sons. He was not a pal-around kind of guy, not one who would play catch with you in the backyard. Usually at the end of the day he was spent, with the best of himself left behind at the office. And even at his best at the office, he was fairly aloof to me anyway.

Ron was just the opposite. He may have sensed in me a need to connect with an older man. That year Ron took me backpacking up to the top of Mt. Whitney. On that trip we saw a lot of amazing sights on our way to what seemed to be the top of the world. We talked a lot about science, laughed a lot, and in the process he became a little like a father to me, filling a void that my father was either unable or unwilling—or simply too busy—to fill.

And then the question: "Have you ever thought about flying?"

He had listened to me talk about our trip around the world, listened to my farfetched fantasies of flying jets, my admiration for the pilots who flew them, my desire to use my mind in a profession, my apprehensions about the boredom of sacking sawdust or being stuck in an office doing the same things day in and day out for the rest of my life.

"Have you ever thought about flying?"

The question followed me like a stray, not only for the next few days but for the next few years. His brother Paul, whom I also knew well, had been taking flying lessons and loved it. "Try it," he said. "I think you would be good at it."

It seemed a wish-upon-a-star type aspiration. Something right out of a fairy tale. After all, I was just a kid. And flying was a man's job. Where would I get the training? Where would I get the money for the training?

Ron was thirteen years older than I was, a genius with a near-photographic memory. He was quiet and humble yet had a prodigious grasp of scientific things, which made him fascinating to listen to. Talking with Ron stimulated my inquisitive young mind. I was full of questions, and he was full of answers. Yet he never made me feel stupid for asking or for not knowing something. I respected him. And I took everything he said seriously. But nothing more seriously than the words "Try it. I think you would be good at it."

Ron's brother Paul began to fan the flames of the burning desire to fly that was smoldering under the surface. I feared talking about it with my parents. Mom would be fearful. Dad would be practical. I also feared talking about it with my granddad, whom I adored. He had started the business that I was now a part of. Nothing would please him more than to see me follow in his footsteps. Nothing would disappoint him more than for me to follow another set of footsteps.

It would be another four years, the summer of 1968, before I got up the courage to take my first lesson.

My instructor was a man named Terry, an airline pilot who had given up a safe and secure job as a banker for the adventure of flying. One day I met Terry at Brackett Airfield, bought a pilot's logbook, gave him thirty dollars, and we took off.

I had always been good with machines. I was driving tractors at age ten, then forklifts, then giant Caterpillar front-end loaders, then 18-wheelers. I loved the feel of machines. They felt like an extension of who I was. But no machine prepared me for the Cessna 150 we flew that day.

I sat beside Terry in the cockpit as we flew around the Southern California city of Ontario. It was an oh-my-gosh moment. A moment I never forgot. And a moment that kept me coming back, plunking down another thirty dollars, and another and another, to recapture that thrill.

I felt free when I was flying. Above the fray of traffic. Above the worries of the workaday world. Above the boundaries of stop signs and double lines, signs that signaled No U-turns or Speed Limit 35. Here I was untrammeled by the rules and regulations of everyday life. Here I was free to be me. Here was where I belonged. And I knew it on the first flight.

I learned everything I could as fast as I could. I took as many lessons as I could afford, learning how to taxi, steer the rudders with my feet, take off, guide the aircraft with fingertip pressure on the controls, everything.

Nothing felt as good as being in the cockpit, lifting off from earth, and taking flight. Nothing. And now nothing could stop me from becoming a professional pilot.

I would drive a truck at night, earning a decent income. I took aviation ground school between my afternoon classes and work—went to school during the day—and flew every chance I got in between. After I had taken twenty hours of flight instruction from Terry, I met Chuck and took the rest from him.

Finally, in June 1969, after logging sixty hours in the air, I was ready for my test with the FAA, the regulatory board that issues licenses for pilots. Chuck and I were taking one of our routine flights with a stop in Visalia. It was there we parted ways and I hopped into the Cessna 150 that I had rented for the short fifteen-minute flight to Tulare, where I was scheduled to meet the flight examiner for my private pilot flight test. Chuck had signed me off for a solo flight so I could make the hop to my flight check destination. His last-minute instruction replayed in my mind as I taxied over to the hangar. "Relax, you're more than ready," he had said. "And remember, when he asks a question, just give him the exact answer. No more and no less. And treat him with respect." That's all the advice Chuck gave me. But it proved to be enough.

After I landed the airplane, I taxied to the large former WWII hangar where I was to meet the man who had the power to approve my pilot's license. The examiner was a relaxed fiftyish WWII veteran. We quickly exchanged preliminary information, strapped ourselves into the aircraft, and proceeded with my flight exam. My attention was so focused that it seemed like only moments before we were again landing and taxiing to the hangar. The check ride was over. The examiner shook my hand in congratulations and signed my log book. I was now a licensed pilot.

That was the biggest day of my life. I could fly alone. I was a pilot on my way to living my dream.

"Have you ever thought about flying?" Ron had asked four years before.

And I haven't stopped thinking about it since.

8

SECRET PLACE OF THE MOST HIGH

A shooting pain in my shoulder brought me back to earth.

It was no longer June of '69. It was July. What a difference a month makes.

In the days that followed, friends were still coming by to visit. Now it was more friends from our church and less from school. Howard and Ginny Dunn were two of them. They were friends of our family for a long time and it lifted my spirits to see them.

"How are you doing, Dale?" Howard asked.

"Thankful to be alive and happy to be home."

"I think God gave me a Scripture He wants me to share with you."

What does God have for me? I wondered.

He paused, waiting for my permission.

"Please. Go ahead."

He picked up his Bible and thumbed through its well-worn pages. "Psalm 91," he said, and started reading:

> "He who dwells in the secret place of the Most High
> Shall abide under the shadow of the Almighty.
> I will say of the Lord, He is my refuge and my fortress;
> My God; in Him I will trust.
> Surely He shall deliver you from the snare of the fowler,
> And from the perilous pestilence.

He shall cover you with His feathers,
And under His wings you shall take refuge:
His truth shall be your shield and buckler.
You shall not be afraid of the terror by night;
Nor for the arrow that flies by day,
Nor of the pestilence that walks in darkness,
Nor of the destruction that lays waste at noonday.
A thousand may fall at your side,
And ten thousand at your right hand;
But it shall not come near you.

Psalm 91:1–7"

Tears burned my eyes. I had never heard that before. As he read, it was like the first light of dawn in my spirit, a spirit that had been wandering in the dead of night trying to find answers.

I was alive not because I had been living a good life for Him. To the contrary, I was living my own life for me. I had a deep sense that the prayers of my parents and grandparents over the years had somehow protected me. I wasn't certain, but I thought so. All I was certain of was that it wasn't anything *I* had done.

Why me? was the question that burned within me. And now this psalm shed light on a possible answer. Why was *I* spared? I think it had something to do with God's sovereign purpose. It wasn't only because He loved me. It was because He had plans for me. What those plans were wasn't clear at the time. What was clear was that He had been my fortress against the blunt force trauma that had killed the other pilots. I hit the same dome my friends hit and at the same speed. We all impacted the monument within inches of each other. I needed the strength of a fortress to survive the crash. But I needed the softness of feathers to survive the fall.

Why was I allowed to get on that flight in the first place? If God was providentially protecting me, why not keep me from the accident altogether?

Because I think there were more important things that needed protecting than my physical being or my vocational dreams. The broken bones would lead to a broken spirit. God loved the heart of the little boy I once was. Somewhere along the way to growing up, my heart lost its way. He was turning me back, showing me where I had lost my way, and letting me begin again from where I had started, back in the fifth grade when I surrendered my life to God and invited Jesus into my heart.

It was a piece of the larger puzzle. A big piece. It was what I needed at the moment. Everything wasn't clear, but clear enough that I could take the next step. Which was good, because that's all the strength I had.

I didn't have strength for the entire journey. Just enough for the next step.

The next step landed me in the backyard.

I had wheeled myself there to soak up some summer sun and to read what I could of the Bible my parents had given me at graduation. If God had a plan for me, I wanted to know about it. More important, I wanted to know *Him*.

Even though I was an athlete who had driven trucks and flown planes, traveled the world and achieved a lot of success, there was so much in me that hadn't matured. I had the body of a well-developed man. I had been a body builder. I could walk up and down stairs on my hands, do somersaults off the high dive; I excelled at sports. Yet if you had put a mirror up to my spiritual life, I was the proverbial ninety-eight-pound weakling. I had no spiritual strength, no stamina, nothing at all to rely on in the spiritual realm.

If indeed there is a spiritual battle going on all around us, I was not a warrior but a water boy.

And I didn't want that. I wanted to be a warrior, one of the King's men. But first I had to know the King. And I started getting to know Him that afternoon in the backyard.

I used my good eye to read. The Bible lay on my lap, flopped open. I read as the sunlight danced through the trees, as the wind whispered through its branches, sometimes turning the pages for me. It was so peaceful back there. My life had been so busy chasing my dreams that I never had time like this, just to sit and read and think, to enjoy the warmth of the sun on my arms, the breath of the sky against my face.

I desired a friendship with the God who had spared my life. If I were ever to walk again, it would be with Him on His path, not mine. If I were ever to run again, it would be for Him, on the course He set before me. And if I were ever to fly again, it would be with Him at the controls. He would not be *my* copilot; I would be *His*. Who knows where we would go together; but wherever it was, it would be together. No more flying solo.

It was during these visits with God that I began to realize that if I were ever going to be normal again, God would have to do the miraculous and I would have to do the arduous.

There was a lot of hard work ahead. It would be all uphill with the wind in my face. But I wouldn't be going it alone.

I couldn't really do anything in the way of physical therapy. I was still in casts, a wheelchair, and a lot of pain. Where to start when everything is broken?

I started with my eye. Somehow I got the idea that my damaged eye needed exercise. The doctor had told me I would not regain sight in that eye. At best, I would be able to distinguish light from darkness. Without telling anyone, and when no one was around, I taped my good eye shut and forced myself to use my injured eye.

It was painful at first. I could only see shadows. Light and darkness registered, but nothing else. Day after day I did this. And day after day I thanked Him. I thanked Him for what I saw, and I thanked Him in advance that someday I would see normally again. I clung to the Scripture "For we walk by faith, not by sight" that I found in 2 Corinthians 5:7. It was going to take faith to get my sight back. I wasn't going to get faith by simply praying for it. Faith would come by believing and then acting upon what God said in His Word.

During that time I began to realize that if I was ever going to be normal again, it would require two things: First, the hand of God to perform a series of miracles on my body. And second, an enormous amount of effort on my part.

One day while trying to read the Bible with my injured eye, my brother walked up behind me. I was straining so intently to read that I hadn't noticed him.

"What are you doing, Dale? Why do you have tape over your left eye?"

His questions felt like an inquisition, and I felt like a fool. I wasn't about to explain. My faith was growing, but still I was timid and self-conscious.

"I was just experimenting, that's all. I wanted to see how much I could see with my right eye. I think it's a little better."

"Did you have to tape your good eye shut to find out?" His chiding stung, and he pulled off the tape.

After that I was more careful about doing my exercises. And I was more careful about what I said and to whom I said it. My faith was fragile but growing. As it grew, I began to feel more confident that God was going to heal me, that I would be normal again, that I would walk again, run again, fly again.

Eventually I got to the point where I could go to church. That wasn't something high on my list before the crash. Now it was. It wasn't a religious routine I sought. It was a relationship with the Most High, the Almighty, the One who had been my refuge and my fortress, the One who had delivered me from the snare, who had covered me with His feathers.

God wasn't theoretical anymore. He was personal. And now my relationship with Him was personal.

I had a lot of attention that first Sunday I went back, both from the pulpit and from the pews. But gradually I began to blend in. As I did, I noticed something I had never given a second thought to before. There were other people at church in wheelchairs: a person who had been crippled in an accident, one from a disease, another from a disability. I felt enormous compassion for them, seeing them from the vantage point of someone who was also disabled. I found myself wheeling my way over to them, striking up a conversation, asking about their lives. It was the first time that had ever happened. Sunday after Sunday they had come. And Sunday after Sunday I had ignored them. *How many others have ignored them?* I wondered. How hurtful that must have felt, being marginalized like that. Sitting while everyone else was standing. Listening to fragments of conversations that others were having. No one stooping to talk with you, ask how *you* were doing, let alone ask you over for a meal or out to a movie.

It broke my heart . . . in places I didn't know needed breaking.

9

FEAR AND MEMORY LOSS

Since I couldn't fly yet, I thought it would be a step forward to audit the aviation ground school at a local junior college. Several of my high school peers were attending there, and Anna, my long-time girlfriend, was willing to regularly drive me to the college and even wheel me into the class. I couldn't do much but listen, learn, and use my right hand to turn the pages of my book and take notes. I thought a few sessions would get me thinking in the right direction again.

The instructor took me under his wing and encouraged me in my commitment to aviation. Since everyone in the class was an aspiring pilot, they had all heard about the crash, and I was somewhat of a celebrity. The instructor approached me and asked me to speak to the class about aviation safety. It was a great opportunity to express some of the concerns I'd developed since the crash.

"Intersection departures should not be made for any reason," I began. "The pilot in command should take control immediately if he senses any problems. Learn the FAA regulations—always obey the regulations. . . ." I droned on with my newfound convictions. But before long I found it impossible to stick to my well-rehearsed speech.

Then I remembered the boldness of Peter and John when they answered a disbelieving team of religious leaders who had commanded them not to speak about Jesus anymore. Peter and John answered and said, "Whether it is right in the sight of God to listen to you more than to God, you judge.

For we cannot but speak the things which we have seen and heard" (Acts 4:19–20).

I'm not leaving this classroom without telling these people what God has done for me, I decided. I felt the same overwhelming love in my heart for these students as I did for the hospital staff and the people in the cars on the freeway when I awoke from the coma months earlier. I thought of Chuck Burns, my flight instructor and friend, whom I never told about Jesus. I reflected on the pain and guilt of his eternal loss. These thoughts were enough to stop me in the midst of my "better safe than sorry" message.

"There is only one reason that I am alive and talking to you today . . ." As my eyes flooded with tears, I paused to regain control of my voice. "God saved my life. God loves me very much, but He loves each of you no less. Jesus Christ came into this world to die so that you can live." I looked around the room and noticed that every eye seemed intently focused on me.

"I challenge each of you to read what Jesus said and taught in the Bible. You can do it quickly and easily. Get a red-letter edition of the New Testament, and just read the red letters, the words Jesus spoke. You owe it to yourself to find out if Jesus is the Son of God. He either is or He isn't. You decide. But if you find that He truly is the Son of God, wouldn't you want to learn more about Him?"

I continued, "I've done this exact exercise, and I don't believe for a moment that any mere man, no matter how great or educated, could say and do the things Jesus did. It wouldn't be possible. I challenge you to learn about the free gift of eternal life with God, which you only receive by believing on Jesus Christ. You see, Jesus came into the world not to condemn the world, but that the world through Him might be saved."

As I rolled back to my desk, my classmates erupted first with loud applause, and then a standing ovation. The response only brought more tears to my eyes. But I could tell by the teacher's expression that my lesson was not quite the one he'd had in mind.

A few days later I had another idea. "You want to do *what*?" Mom asked, stopping her dinner preparations.

"I want to go back to Pasadena College. I need to get back into school so I can finish my degree and move on to becoming an airline pilot. The airlines need pilots real bad right now."

I knew she didn't want to discuss my flying again. It had brought her too much pain. So she avoided that part of my statement.

"Dale, it's only been a few months since the crash. You need to get stronger before you tackle a goal like that. How would you get around? How would you carry your books, get up the stairs, and accomplish all the other things you'd need to do? You're still in a wheelchair, and you've only got one arm to wheel yourself around."

"I'm stronger now, Mom. Besides, I feel I need to tell my friends about the changes God has made in my life. It might help them."

"You were pretty rebellious when you were there before," she said.

"Well, yeah. I didn't exactly like all the rules."

"You don't have to like them; you just have to follow them."

"How much trouble can a guy in a wheelchair get into? Look at me."

She smiled. And she talked to Dad. My parents made some calls; I wrote a letter and had a tearful meeting with Dr. Shelburne Brown, the president of the college, who saw the change in me, and Dr. Lewis Thompson, the dean of students, who was especially kind and understanding. Dr. Thompson went above and beyond the call of duty, helping make arrangements for my return.

It was October when I returned, and classes had already started. Getting around was a pain. Still as stubborn as ever, I usually refused help. It didn't matter how many books I had to carry, how many flights of stairs I had to hop up with my one good leg, I was going to do this. I was late for every class, sopping wet with sweat, and could hardly concentrate. I had trouble following the teacher, trouble taking notes, trouble remembering the notes I had taken.

I had been something of a big man on campus before the crash, and

I expected to be an even bigger man, commanding even more attention after it. But the old crowd I used to hang out with began to thin. After all, I was in a wheelchair, wrapped in bandages, and weighed down with casts. I wasn't as mobile as I used to be, wasn't as fun as I used to be. On top of that, I was pretty off-putting to look at. And I wasn't sporting around in my MGB, giving rides to my buddies.

I had experienced a lot of things on that campus, but this was the first time I experienced loneliness. It hurt, especially when the same people that had sought me out before were now seeking ways to avoid me.

Even my former college roommate avoided me. I could hardly blame him, but I could also hardly bear it.

My entire identity had been built around the physical, from body building to athletics to my appearance. Because of those things, I had an aura of attractiveness about me. Now the aura was gone, and I was alone.

As I was wheeling myself across campus, feeling a little sorry for myself, I heard a small plane flying overhead. I was gripped with an unexpected longing. *I've got to get out of this wheelchair and back in the sky,* I thought. *I don't care how beat-up my body is, I'm going to be a pilot again. Someday. Nothing is going to stop me!*

I stopped in my tracks and wheeled myself to the first pay phone I could find. I called Capt. Fred Griffith, a veteran professional pilot I had become acquainted with. He had been a test pilot for Lockheed Aircraft and was one of the best instructors in the country. Fred was a true aviator. He also knew something of what I was going through. Years earlier he had had his own brush with death. He ejected from a test flight, and his parachute failed to open properly. He survived the fall but was severely injured. He knew firsthand the fear of flying after an accident. *Who better to turn to?* I thought.

I told him of my desire to get back into flying again and particularly to fly over the air memorial that we had crashed into. "But I don't want anyone else to know," I told him. I asked if he would fly with me, and he agreed.

The next day I managed somehow to get to the airport. I shouldn't have been driving, but I was desperate. And desperate people do desperate things. Fred met me there and wheeled me out to his single engine Cessna 182. I hadn't been back at the terminal since the day of the crash. Rolling up to the terminal, I saw the sign over the large glass entry: *Pacific Aeromotive*. Seeing it, I had a strange, unsettled feeling.

Fred helped me into the cockpit, and I perched in the left seat, feeling cramped and awkward.

"Would you like to conduct the Before Start Checklist?" Fred asked.

I stared at the instrument panel with all its dials and levers, and for the first time I realized I had no idea how to operate them.

I started to read the checklist out loud. "Flap handle."

I paused. I couldn't remember what a flap handle was. I had arrived at the airport believing I was capable of piloting the Cessna 182. After all, I had my pilot's license and had even finished training for my multiengine rating. But as I scanned the dials and levers, everything looked foreign to me. I felt like it was the first time I'd ever been in the cockpit of an airplane. I simply couldn't remember how to fly! Two years of information and experience had been wiped from my mind.

Fred patiently went over the checklist and then started the engine. When it roared to life, I felt out of control. I wanted to stop and do it another day. My heart was pounding so hard I could barely hear Fred speak. Fred had wanted to let me make the takeoff, but he changed his mind when he saw how fearful I was.

"Relax, Dale. I'll do the flying. You just sit back and enjoy the ride."

Fred taxied the Cessna down to Runway 15, just as we had done the day of the crash. He pushed the engines full throttle and took off, just as we had done the day of the crash.

It was so traumatic I could hardly breathe. We ascended rapidly, and in the blink of an eye we were soaring over the dome-shaped monument. My heart pounded and my forehead dripped with sweat as I watched the Portal of the Folded Wings disappear beneath us.

"You did it, Dale! Congratulations!" he said. "Is that going to do it for you?" Then he looked at me. I had a white-knuckled grip on the seat and my shirt was soaked in sweat.

"Are you going to be alright?"

I was at a loss for words and an even greater loss of confidence. Finally I spoke. "I'd like you to land and then go around once again, Fred, if that's OK with you. The sooner I get over this, the better."

Fred understood. But the second time around was no easier. I was limp with terror. I couldn't move, I couldn't engage. I felt so ashamed. *Go on,* I told myself. *Get over it. It's like getting thrown off a horse. You've got to get back on and ride or you'll never overcome the fear.*

When we landed, I was relieved but embarrassed. I felt like I had let Capt. Fred down. He told me my reaction was normal for what I had been through and reassured me that I would conquer my fears. I just had to keep facing them.

And that's what I was determined to do. The next day I made arrangements to enroll in the aviation ground school at the nearby junior college—the same course I had audited and where I had spoken to fellow students. It would help me relearn what I had forgotten. The next class started in mid-January, which would give me a little more time to recover.

Shortly after the flight with Fred, I dropped out of Pasadena College.

Mom was right. It was too much, too soon.

And it was too lonely.

(10)

A FUTURE AND A HOPE

The remainder of the fall of 1969 was even lonelier. I had become disillusioned with my friendships, which one by one fell away during that season of my life. I became weary of the well-wishers, the Hallmark-card greetings, the hang-in-there sentiments. I became suspicious of the smiles, the promises to come and see me that never materialized, and the call-me-if-you-need-anything good-byes.

One friendship, however, didn't disappoint. I looked forward to time alone with God—reading my Bible, praying, thinking, which I did a lot in our backyard, our suddenly leafless backyard.

Up till then, I had always been a doer; now I was learning just to be. Not that I really had a choice in the matter. It was as if there had been an untimely frost and the seasons changed overnight. I went from the summertime of my life to the dead of winter without so much as a storm warning.

Someone once said, I forget who, "In October, when the leaves fall, you can see deeper into the forest." It's true. So much foliage had fallen from my branching ambitions, and as a result, I *could* see deeper into the forest that was my life.

I didn't feel I needed to be doing anything—playing among the trees or gathering firewood or trying to find some way of making money out of the forest. I could just be there and rest. It was good. It was part of my restoration.

Trees need the winter. I never knew that before. They need time to strengthen for the growth they experience in springtime. All that green, pulpy growth has to harden, or the tree would not be able to withstand the seasonal winds that whip against it.

I had experienced a lot of growth. Now was the time for the energy to be diverted from the branches to the roots. The roots of my faith were going deeper. Much of what was going on with me was going on underground, so to speak, beneath the surface, unseen.

Growth can be a lonely place, but it is a necessary place.

That's what I learned in the fall of '69, there in my wheelchair, in the backyard with the bare branches—and my Bible.

Initially my parents, as well as my doctor, had not revealed the full extent of my injuries. They told me things like "your ankle is broken" or "your shoulder is dislocated" or "your back is broken in a few places." But they never went into detail. Later I learned that Dr. Graham had advised my parents not to discuss my injuries with me until I asked. In this way, he believed I would learn of their seriousness as I was emotionally able to handle the information.

I had been talking about and praying about my physical restoration for several weeks, when my dad sat down with me for a man-to-man talk.

"You've got a lot of work ahead of you, Dale. And you need to understand that it may be years before you'll be able to function normally, even somewhat normally. You'll not be able to regain the use of everything, you know. The doctor says you'll never walk again."

I wasn't prepared for what he said and couldn't respond.

He explained, "We didn't want to tell you everything too soon. You had enough trauma those first few weeks."

I don't know if it was for my benefit or his, but I said, "Don't worry, Dad. It will all come back. You'll see. God will restore me to the way I was. And on the anniversary of the crash, I'm going to fly over that monument as pilot in command. With God's help we'll do it. He and I are a team now. Just wait, you'll see."

Dad sat back in his chair and said nothing, which was uncharacteristic of him. He had always been a can-do kind of guy, always looking on the bright side. But Dad had been apprehensive about my flying. It wasn't a career choice he could fully support. And now, after the crash, he could muster no enthusiasm at all. He couldn't even fake it.

That was the last time I spoke to him about flying over the monument, the last time I spoke to him about a lot of things.

Ever since my release from the hospital, we had been making numerous trips to Burbank for additional surgeries, postoperative checkups, and treatments. Day after day we threaded our way along the freeways to Dr. Graham's office, located just across the street from St. Joseph. We averaged three trips a week. Then we were down to two.

On one of those visits in early November, my grandparents joined my parents and I to talk with Dr. Graham together. First there was the usual routine of X rays, and then the doctor examined my eye, head, face, back, legs, and ankles. Then we waited in the lobby for the X rays to come out.

When Dr. Graham called us in to his office that day, he was unusually animated as he pointed to my X rays. "I can't believe this," he said.

"Praise the Lord!" Grandpa declared under his breath as he characteristically rattled the coins in his pocket.

I wheeled myself in for a closer look. "What's going on?" I asked.

Dad spoke first. "Dale, when the doctors examined you at the hospital, they told us your left ankle was so severely shattered it would never heal properly. The bone had exploded on impact. Without blood circulation, there is no healing."

"It's called *avascular necrosis,*" the doctor said. "It means bone death."

Dad continued. "The doctors recommended operating on your ankle to remove the shattered bone and move your foot up against your leg bone, supporting it with metal braces and pins. That way you could still put weight on your foot. The only problem is your left leg would be three or four inches shorter than your right leg. You'd have to wear an elevated shoe, and without an ankle joint, you would have a severe limp."

A chill crept through me as he spoke. I had no idea such a possibility existed. I shivered at the thought.

"Your grandpa and I talked it over," my dad said, "we prayed about it, and we felt we should give God an opportunity to work in the situation."

Dr. Graham listened as my dad spoke, his face reflecting no emotion. Then he interjected, "The risk was that once the bone died, it would likely collapse. We would not be able to do anything at that point. And you would be unable to walk at all. Ever. From my perspective, it was a big gamble."

Tears filled my eyes. "So what did you find on the X rays today?"

"The bone has begun to vascularize," the doctor said. "For some reason blood is beginning to circulate. The bone is beginning to heal." He looked at the X rays and shook his head. "I can't explain it, but here it is."

"Praise the Lord!" Grandpa said again, a little more emphatically.

You can imagine the ride home. We were all filled with joy—and gratitude. As the familiar green freeway signs flew past, the visual of a checklist came to mind:

1. God spared me from certain death.
2. My vision is changed. Nothing looks the same to me.
3. God has given me a renewed spirit.
4. There are no internal injuries.
5. I was released from the hospital in eight days.
6. Now God is healing my dead ankle.

There is a pattern here, I thought. *God is doing something. Even the crazy idea to exercise my eye is part of it.*

With that thought, I closed my left eye. It was true. The vision in my injured eye was becoming clearer.

My faith was doing handstands. I could hardly contain myself. That's when I prayed, *God, I'm going to get to know You better. I'm going to work with You to get the job done that You have in mind for my life. I don't know what Your plan is exactly, but I have a feeling it's something special. I'll tell You this: I'm going to stick close enough to You to find out exactly what it is.*

11

SURVIVING THE UNSURVIVABLE

It was late November. I had to get out—out of the backyard, out of the house, out of town. I asked a friend to take me to the Portal of the Folded Wings in Burbank.

I had to see it again, this time up close and personal. I had to see the place where my pilot friends had died and where I had lost so much of my life, so much of my memory. Maybe something would come back. An image. A feeling. A missing piece to the puzzle my life had become.

We drove to North Hollywood, where Valhalla Memorial Park Cemetery was located, just off the flight path of Runway 15. After we parked, I eased into the wheelchair, and my friend wheeled me to the memorial.

The closer we got, the larger it loomed.

The larger it loomed, the smaller I felt.

It was massive, a huge cube of a building topped with a colorful dome. As we approached it, I saw a large bronze plaque that read:

WELCOME TO THIS SHRINE OF
AMERICAN AVIATION.
THE PLAQUES HEREIN MARK
THE FINAL RESTING PLACE
OF PIONEERS IN FLIGHT.

On each side there were sculpted cherubs and female figures lifting their hands skyward. It felt strangely comforting, this lifing of hands. My prayers to God were for clarity about the crash. They were questions I raised to Him. I came empty-handed. Would I leave the same way? I didn't expect all my questions to be answered, but I expected to leave with something.

We looked at the dome. The place of impact was still being repaired. I didn't say much that day, but I did a lot of thinking. *The FAA classified our accident as non-survivable.*

At that moment I asked God, *Did I survive only to find out that I caused the accident, the deaths of Chuck and Gene? Will that be the outcome, once the investigation is complete? Do I need to learn to live with the guilt and the shame? How can I live with it? How can I move on? Was it a blessing that I lived, or a curse? Perhaps the investigation will reveal I wasn't to blame, I wasn't at all responsible. Perhanps the crash was caused either by mechanical or pilot error.*

As we got closer, I saw another plaque identifying the Italian-American artist who created the sculptures and ornamentation:

Frederico Augustino Giorgi
PORTAL SCULPTOR
1878–1963

I later learned the sculptor considered this work to be his masterpiece. It was beautiful in one sense. In another sense, it was grotesque—a hulk of a building standing so stoically; an immovable object that had snatched our plane out of the sky and threw it to the ground. An unchanging structure that forever changed three lives. Without apology or the slightest show of remorse.

We went inside to see plaques of remembrance for the fallen pioneers of aviation. The ashes of fifteen of them were buried there. Sensing I needed time to process my thoughts, my friend left me alone. I looked up to see that the dome was a mosaic of stars—a portal to the heavens. All of my thoughts were drawn there, all my empty-handed prayers.

The questions that had hounded me before, the ones I thought had been held at bay, came back at me in a vicious assault.

Why did I live? Why me and not the others? Why, God?

I sat beneath the dome of stars, wondering with my questions, waiting for His answers.

Was I spared because God had a special plan for me? *Is that true, God? Do You? Did You save me so I could serve You? God, almost all of my friends have left me. I am no longer popular. I'm the guy in the wheelchair who survived "that crash." I can't play sports. I can't remember what was said in class, no matter how hard I try. How am I going to do this, God? How am I going to go through life with this limp body and this lame brain?*

I paused, waiting for something, unsure what it was. Was I waiting for one of the angels on the shrine to come down and explain it all? Was I hoping for heaven to open and spill out the answers like gum balls? Was I waiting for a sign? A word? An audible voice? An inner conviction? I had no idea. Not even a clue.

But I was there. I showed up. And I was there with my one hand raised to heaven. I was not one to beg, but I was begging. *I've never known loneliness before, God. Is this a season in my life when You want it to be just You and me? If so, just say so. I'll be fine if that's what You want. Is that what You want? Please, do something, say something. Anything. Just don't leave me alone.*

During those weeks I made many visits to the memorial, by myself mostly. Sometimes I would get in the car and drive there at night. The cemetery was closed at night, and I would drag my bent and broken body to the fence, crawl under it, casts and all, in order to spend a few hours alone there. I prayed there, flat on my back, looking up at the dome. I thought there, trying to dredge up something from my subconscious. And I cried there. For Chuck. For Gene. For the robust person I once was. For the shell of a person I was now.

Dale and the Piper Aztec that he and Chuck flew regularly before the crash. Photo taken November 1969.

I think I used the memorial as a focal point to help get my memory back.

Doctors who worked on me talked with me only briefly about my memory loss. Dr. Graham didn't seem as concerned with it as with the other losses I had suffered. Maybe it was because he felt he could help with the ankle and the shoulder and the face but not with the memory.

Doctors explained that there are different types of amnesia. The two most common are retrograde and anterograde. The former type involves memory loss before the cause, such as a motorcyclist not remembering driving his motorcycle prior to his head injury. The latter has to do with the inability to store new memories after the cause, such as the motorcyclist not being able to recall his hospital experiences or conversations with family and friends who visited him there.

Posttraumatic amnesia, which affects memory before and after head trauma, can be transient or permanent, depending on the severity of the brain damage. Some of my memory loss has proven to be permanent, some of it transient.

The transient losses return at the oddest times and in the oddest ways, with no particular pattern. The memories are random. *When* they return and *why* they return are also random.

The depth and duration of this kind of amnesia are related to how severe the injury is. Often people with head trauma may remember events, but they will not remember the faces of the people in the events. Another type of amnesia, called source amnesia, is when people can recall certain information, but they don't know where or how they obtained the information.

Since different parts of the brain store different types of memories, the more pervasive the damage, the more types of memories are affected. All this to say I suffered a lot of damage and as a result experienced a lot of memory loss.

At the memorial that November day when my friend took me, I still had no memory of the crash. No memory of the three days in a coma. There were only sketchy memories of people and events in my past. There were no words from heaven. No answers. But it was important for me to be there. I'm glad I went. Something had drawn me there—it was almost a gravitational pull. I felt as if I were some small, inconsequential planet orbiting closer and closer to the sun, and the closer I got the more of me was being burned away.

Somehow—in ways I can't understand, let alone express—it felt good. Cleansing. Cathartic. And in some way necessary.

I would be back.

And I would keep going back until the shrine gave up the secret it was keeping.

Or until I was burned away completely.

⑫

GOOD NEWS AND BAD NEWS

The crash was almost six months behind me now. I had faithfully made the pilgrimage to Dr. Graham's office more times than I could count. They were mostly routine visits. Routine X rays. Routine checks to see how I was healing, how I was holding up.

Today was different. Today he brought out the usual X rays, but he said something most unusual. "Well, Dale, I've got good news and bad news."

I perked up, all ears.

"The good news is that your ankle is doing surprisingly well."

"Great," I said. "What's the bad news?"

"Well, it's not really news to us, but it will be to you. It's your shoulder." Dr. Graham looked me straight in the eye, as if to see how I would take the news.

"My shoulder? I know that I can't move my arm now, but it's going to be OK someday, isn't it? It was just dislocated, right?"

"It wasn't dislocated, Dale, it was disintegrated. In fact, on the medical report I described your ball-and-socket joint as having exploded. We even found shoulder bone throughout your back, neck, and chest. It had blown to bits. And the muscles and ligaments all around that area were stretched way beyond their elasticity."

"So that's why I can't lift my arm."

"That's exactly why. When we did the surgeries, we put all the pieces of the bone back together the best we could. We hoped that eventually you might gain some mobility. At this point, I'm pessimistic. You have no strength in that shoulder, and no control of it. We hoped by now you would. Not only that, Dale, but your shoulder muscles have been inactive for almost six months now. In that amount of time, injured, unused muscles grow brittle. Before much longer, you'll have virtually no chance of ever using your shoulder and most of your arm again."

Not the news I was prepared to hear. Questions raced through my mind. *What about my plans for flying, for ground school, for flight instruction?*

"So, what can we do?" I asked tentatively.

Dr. Graham spoke enthusiastically now. "If we can go back a third time into the left shoulder area and take out some more slack muscle, I think you might have a 10 percent chance of lifting your arm about 45 degrees someday. That's the best we can hope for, Dale."

My heart sank. "Ten percent?" I took a deep breath and with it came a surge of faith. "Well, Doc, a ten percent chance of success is ten percent more than God needs. Let's go for it."

Dr. Graham looked at me soberly. "OK. There really is no other choice. The muscles are deteriorating rapidly. To tell you the truth, I'm very concerned about what we're going to find when we get in there. It could be too late."

Dr. Graham had only one date open for surgery. If I didn't take it, I would have to wait another month, which he thought was perilously late.

This will be the last *operation,* I vowed to myself. But I had made that same vow so many operations before. I had already had twelve surgeries, and here I was agreeing to go under the knife again.

When I checked in to St. Joseph Hospital, the staff was eager to see me, see the progress I had made, and was ready to help me get through the next phase of my recovery. In spite of the cheerful staff, the place had been a prison to me, a place of pain and shadows and horrible memories. I arrived as late as I could.

When I got to my room, I noticed the curtains were drawn between me and my roommate. It wasn't long before I learned why.

"Nurse!" an angry voice blurted out. "Get in here! Can you hear me? Nurse!"

When the nurse came in, you could see the weariness on her face from having to answer endless calls like this from the crabby old man. He rattled off a litany of complaints: Dinner was cold. The meat was tough. Everything tasted bland. The TV wasn't working right. The volume was set too low. Then another diatribe about his medication.

Congratulations, Dale, I thought. *You've got yourself a real winner this time.* I wondered whether I would have to put up with this all night.

Then, unexpectedly, the gentlest of thoughts came into my mind. I began to wonder about this man, his life, where he was spiritually. I wondered why he was so angry. An overwhelming love for him came over me and I felt compelled to speak to him. I prayed silently for him. Then I maneuvered myself out of bed, let go of the railing, and hopped across the room. I grabbed the curtain that separated us and wiggled it.

"Hello, sir," I said. "What's your name?"

The pause stretched for what seemed an eternity. Then he spoke, his words bristling with irritation.

"Name's Green. Jocl Green."

"Well, my name is Dale Black, Mr. Green. I guess we'll be sharing the same room. Nice to meet you."

He pulled back the curtain. A leathery, saddlebag of a face glared at me. "What are you in the hospital for? You're just a kid."

I chuckled. "Yeah, I don't know if you remember a plane crash back in July . . ."

I went on to give him the short version of the story. He did, in fact, recall hearing about it on the news. And he recalled one of the headlines in the newspaper: "Fate? Coincidence? or Cruel Irony?" We talked about the aircraft, about the monument, and about the miracle of my surviving. And then I just blurted it out . . .

"Mr. Green, do you know Jesus Christ? He's the reason I'm alive. He has given me joy like I never knew before. I have purpose in my life now, Mr. Green. Do you know Jesus as your Lord and Savior?"

He looked away. No answer.

"Mr. Green, do you know about the free gift of salvation through Jesus Christ?"

Silence. Then a softening of the face. Then tears. Lots and lots of tears. At last he spoke.

"I'm a minister's son." His voice trembled. "I'm seventy-seven years old, and I've been running from God all my life." He sniffed in the emotion and said with sadness in his voice, "It's too late for me now, Dale."

"It's never too late, Mr. Green. It's never too late to allow God to take your life and turn it into something beautiful. God's time is now. Let's get forgiveness for the past mistakes. God says in His Word that when you ask Him to forgive you, your sins are thrown away, as far as the east is from the west. In other words, He forgets them! It's great, Mr. Green. Give God your life now and you'll forever be glad you did."

Again, silence. I wondered about his reaction, wondered if I had been too bold, too brash. But the love I had for him was overwhelming, just like the love I had for people the first week after the crash. A lot was at stake, I thought. *Everything* was at stake.

At last, I spoke again: "Mr. Green, would you like to pray to God now and ask Him to forgive you?"

Again, silence. Then softly, "I, eh . . . I'd like that."

Mr. Green didn't quite know what to say, I sensed that. I also sensed that the walls of bitterness were coming down. I wasn't quite sure what to do next, what to say, or how to say it. I wasn't experienced at things like this.

"Just repeat after me, Mr. Green."

He nodded, and I just relaxed and tried not to get in the way of what God wanted to do.

"Dear God." He repeated after me. "I'm sorry I've been running away from You." And he repeated that too. "I should have been running *to*

You." He continued, word for word. "Lord, I'm a sinner, and I'm tired of running."

As soon as those words came from his mouth, he broke down and wept, then sobbed. I waited until the tears ran their course.

"Father," I said.

"Father," he said.

"Thank You for Your unending love."

"Thank You for Your unending love."

"And for sending Your Son to die on the cross for me."

"And for sending Your Son to die on the cross for me."

"I invite Jesus into my life right now."

"I invite Jesus into my life right now."

"Take over the controls of my life."

"Take over the controls of my life."

"Thank You, God. Amen."

"Thank You, God. Amen."

He dried his tears, thanked me, and we talked awhile until the nurse came to check on him. I could tell by how he treated her that he was a changed man. The nurse could tell too. He was polite and gentle with her. And with me. After she left, he told me to call him by his first name. "Joel," he reminded me. We talked into the night and became friends. More than friends . . . buddies.

Bright and early in the morning I was prepped for surgery. Joel's side of the room was quiet, and I didn't disturb him. I was wheeled away. The last thing I remember is the nurse giving me a needle in the hip, and my words, which this nurse was used to hearing from me: "Carol, did I tell you that this is my last surgery?" She smiled. The smiled blurred. And I was out.

"Wake up, Dale! Dale, wake up!" Dr. Graham was patting me firmly on the face. When at last I opened my eyes, he was smiling down at me. "Dale, listen! I can hardly believe it! There was no deterioration in your shoulder muscles at all. I had little to do but shorten the muscles. They were healthier than I could ever have imagined." The doctor was so excited he couldn't contain himself. "I think you may eventually have up to 45 degrees mobility out of that shoulder. I can hardly believe it!"

"No, Doc," I managed to say in my groggy state. "My . . . God . . . is a God . . . of completeness. . . . He *will* . . . restore my shoulder. I'll be able to lift my arm over my head someday. You watch. You'll see."

When I was finally wheeled back to my room, I added my shoulder to the list of wonders that God had performed in my life.

A nurse came in to fluff my pillow and pull a blanket over me. I glanced over to say hello to Joel. His bed was empty.

"Hey, where's my buddy?" I asked, motioning to the other side of the room.

The nurse shook her head. "Joel's gone, Dale. I'm sorry. He died early this morning."

I was stunned. My breath left me. My thoughts left me. Then it hit me. Joel was in heaven. And I wasn't sad. I vowed then and there never to be timid about sharing the Good News of Jesus Christ again.

Suddenly I realized another reason why I was in the hospital. I thought of how intricate and complete God's love truly is.

It wasn't just for me and my shoulder.

It was also for Joel.

⑬
FROM HORRIFIC TO HEAVENLY

In March 1970, I re-enrolled at Pasadena College, attending classes during the day. It was there in the dorm, around 2 a.m. on the sixteenth that I awoke with a start, drenched in sweat. The dream was so vivid that for several seconds I thought it was real. I was in the cockpit of the Navajo just as it slammed into the monument at an incredible speed. I was hurled through the air, falling several stories to the ground. My arms whirled violently in circles, trying to keep my balance so I would land on my feet. Before hitting the ground, I woke up.

I had had this dream before—probably a hundred times. This time it was different. This time I felt it. I heard it, I smelled it, and I tasted it. The noise of the crash hurt my ears. The smell of burning oil filled my nostrils. The heat from the engines burned my flesh, and the taste of concrete filled my mouth. It was all so real. I was actually trying to spit pieces of concrete and marble from my mouth as I woke up. The smell lingered in my nose.

I lay in my bed, terrified. I sat up and looked across the room at my roommate to see if the sound of the crash had wakened him, but he was fast asleep. I had to get up. I had to get out of there. It was too intense.

I put on a heavy jacket, got my crutches, and maneuvered myself to the nearby football field. When I reached the 50-yard line, I put down my crutches and eased onto my back. Looking up at the stars, I paused to catch my breath. The starry sky seemed so immense, the glittering wonder of it all blinking down on me. This time, though, was different from the other times I had gone there to process my life. This time it felt as if God were reaching down to me, trying to speak through the silence.

I had prayed so long for God to restore my memory. Was He at last beginning to answer that prayer? It felt like He was. And part of it felt reassuring. Another part felt unsettling. The crash had been horrific. And every cell within me, every space between the cells, had experienced the trauma. My body had become a projectile, traveling at 135 mph, and then stopping suddenly. Abruptly. Violently. And after the initial impact there was another—the seventy-foot free fall to the ground.

Nothing more came that night.

The next night, though, in the very same bed, more of my memory came back to me. I had been asleep and woke up with a start. Sitting up, I remembered some of the names of the people who had come by the hospital, names I had forgotten. My memory was coming back in fragments. I couldn't control when they came, how many came, or in what order they came.

The third night I remembered loading the plane the day of the crash. I recalled that we had performed two engine run-ups that day. I remembered the sound of the engines screaming at high rpms with the propellers out of sync. I remembered Chuck yelling at the last moment while trying to correct the erratic pitch of the plane.

When the memories started coming back, they came back with a heightened sense of awareness. I felt the bumps in the ambulance ride, for instance. I heard the desperate wail of the siren. I smelled aviation fuel everywhere. In the ambulance, the smell of fuel was almost suffocating.

I saw myself inside the ambulance. Then suddenly, I was outside the ambulance, chasing it. Chasing it for what seemed forever. I remember the stark terror I felt on that ride. It was too much for me. It was just too much.

The fourth night I couldn't sleep for fear of what I would remember. I called my parents, telling them I needed to talk. I was so overwhelmed by the horror of the memories that I didn't know what to do. We arranged to meet at a restaurant near the college, but during the time it took for them to make the drive, I had second thoughts. The memories were too raw, I was too fragile to recount them, and I wasn't sure they could help anyway. By the time they arrived, I decided not to share any of it.

On the fifth night the memories returned. This time they were stronger. This time I was leaving my body and floating just below the ceiling in the emergency room. I hadn't remembered it at the time it happened. I remembered it now. And in vivid detail.

Now it was clear these were not dreams, because they were now coming to me while I was wide awake.

During the following week I remembered something so amazing it took my breath away. Images of heaven started coming back. Images and sounds. Sounds and feelings. In the order that they happened. And in intricate detail.

Before the crash I had thought of myself as a realist and a pragmatist, much like my father. I loved science and statistics and things you could touch, hold, quantify, and contain. So my initial reaction to my journey to heaven was one of questioning. But in my heart there was no doubt about it. Whether I liked it or not, the memories were real, and they continued to pour back.

Finally everything started making sense. So many questions were answered. Although my mind had been unable to remember the experiences of leaving my body and visiting the entrance of heaven, my heart had remembered everything, storing it deep within me for the right time to reveal it.

Now was the time.

Gradually the rapid recall slowed. Within a few weeks it was down to a trickle. The picture became clear as each piece of the puzzle was turned over and put into place.

My experiences in heaven, as I have come to understand them, were embedded in me, almost like a memory chip. I say that because they have become so much more than memories. They have become permanent, life-changing events that have reprogrammed my values, my beliefs, the very way I live my life.

Just as it was time for the memories to come back to me, now is the time for them to be shared with you.

14

JOURNEY TO HEAVEN

I kept waking up. And I kept coming back to midfield. If ever there was a field of dreams, that football field in the middle of the night was it. It was the place where my most wonderful and horrible memories collided at the 50-yard line.

My last memories were when I had been in the hospital, seeing myself in the operating room from a vantage point near the ceiling. I remember feeling lighter and lighter, being drawn down the hallway and swept out the door of the hospital, and then suddenly I was gone.

The first memory of where I had gone when I was in a coma made no sense to me. It was a looping memory that replayed itself over and over again. The memory was of this stunningly beautiful light that permeated everything, going out in every direction but not expanding.

How could it be? I wondered. *How could light do that? I've never seen light like that.* My mind refused to cooperate. What I was seeing defied logic, defied rational analysis, let alone rational explanation.

Something was beginning to reveal itself, I was sure of that. I didn't know exactly what, but I did know that my prayers were being answered. God *was* restoring my memory. At first the memories came in fragments, then in a flood. Unlike the earlier memories, which came out of sequence, the memories I am about to share came back sequentially.

These are not memories I could summon on command. They bypassed my conscious brain. If I thought too much, they resisted revealing themselves.

I had to let my brain relax and allow my heart to take over. I wasn't used to giving up control easily, but I had no alternative. They wouldn't come if I didn't let go and tune in to my heart.

So I would go and lie down in the middle of our football field, in the middle of the night, gazing at the starry wonder of the Milky Way, where I would relax, let go, and . . .

Now it was coming back . . . where I had gone.

The more it came back, the more I let go, until the memories replayed themselves like one long, continuous movie.

Leaving the hospital, I sped through what appeared to be a narrow pathway. An incandescent-like beam of light, almost like a searchlight, originated from me and illuminated my path. It wasn't a tunnel of light that I was traveling through. It was a path in the darkness that was delineated by the light. Outside of this pathway was total darkness.

But in the darkness millions of tiny spheres of light zoomed past as I traveled through what looked like deep space, almost as if a jet were flying through a snowstorm at night, its lights reflecting off the flakes as they blurred past.

The speed at which I traveled was blinding, and the path narrowed to twice the width of my body. I had no pain, no discomfort whatsoever. No high-altitude ear-popping. No queasy stomach. No headache. And I had no worries, not even the least concern. Only questions.

What happened to me? Why is this happening to me? Where am I going? What is going to happen next?

What happened next is beyond my ability to describe. I will use the best words I can, yet the best words pale in the presence of what I experienced.

I was still traveling at enormous speed, all the while feeling no sensation of movement. No wind in my hair. No g-forces distorting my face. No pressure against my eyes, making them close.

At this time, I became aware that I was not traveling alone. Accompanying me were two angelic escorts dressed in seamless white garments woven with silver threads. They had no discernible gender but appeared masculine and larger than I was. Their skin tone was light golden brown and their hair fairly short. I could see their emotions, clearly delighted to be ushering me through this wonderland. They moved just behind me, one to the left of me, one to the right. Remarkably, my peripheral vision was enhanced, and I could see both of their glowing faces at the same time. I could even see behind me while hardly moving my head.

I was fast approaching a magnificent city, golden and gleaming among a myriad of resplendent colors. The light I saw was the purest I had ever seen. And the music was the most majestic, enchanting, and glorious I had ever heard.

I was still approaching the city, but now I was slowing down. Like a plane making its final approach for landing. I knew instantly that this place was entirely and utterly holy. Don't ask me how I knew, I just knew. I was overwhelmed by its beauty. It was breathtaking. And a strong sense of belonging filled my heart; I never wanted to leave. Somehow I knew I was made for this place and this place was made for me. Never had I felt so "right" anywhere. For the first time in my life, I was completely "whole."

The entire city was bathed in light, an opaque whiteness in which the light was intense but diffused. In that dazzling light every color imaginable seemed to exist and—what's the right word?—*played*. If joy could be given colors, they would be these colors. The colors were pure and innocent, like children playing in a fountain, splashing, chasing each other, gurgling with laughter. Water everywhere sparkled in the sunshine.

The colors seemed to be alive, dancing in the air. I had never seen so many different colors. If the brightest light on earth could shine through the most magnificent chandelier with tens of thousands of flawless crystals, it would appear as dirty glass in comparison to the amazing brightness and colors that entranced me.

It was breathtaking to watch. And I could have spent forever doing just that. The closer I got to the city, the more distinct the illumination became. The magnificent light I was experiencing emanated from about forty or fifty miles within the city wall.

I saw a great phosphorescent display of light that narrowed to a focal point that was brighter than the sun. Oddly, it didn't make me squint to look at it. And all I wanted to do was to look at it. The light was palpable. It had substance to it, weight and thickness, like nothing I had ever seen before or since.

The light from a hydrogen bomb is the closest I can come to describing it. Just after the bomb is detonated—but before the fireball that forms the mushroom cloud—there is a millisecond of light that flashes as the bomb releases its energy. It was something like that but much larger.

The glow and energy of this light radiated in all directions, upward and outward. It wasn't something you shielded your eyes from; it wasn't something you even flinched at. Just the opposite. It was warm and inviting. Almost hypnotic in its ability to draw you in to it.

Somehow I knew that light and life and love were connected and inter-related. It was as if the very heart of God lay open for everyone in heaven to bask in its glory, to warm themselves in its presence, to bathe in its almost liquid properties so they could be restored, renewed, refreshed.

Remarkably, the light didn't shine *on* things but *through* them. Through the grass. Through the trees. Through the wall. And through the people who were gathered there.

There was a huge gathering of angels and people, millions, countless millions. They were gathered in a central area that seemed over ten miles in diameter. The expanse of people was closer to an ocean than a concert hall. Waves of people, moving in the light, swaying to the music, worshiping God. Holiness hovered over them the way I imagine the Spirit of God brooding over the surface of the deep at the beginning of time. During priceless moments of worship you are so enraptured by it that you don't miss the moment before or long for the moment after.

Somehow the music in heaven calibrated everything, and I felt that nothing was rushed. Nothing waited for you, because you weren't late for anything. You weren't early either, having to wait for what was to happen next. Everything happened right when it was supposed to happen, and you were right there to experience it. In sync. With everything. Never hurried or stressed.

Time was clearly evident. But it, too, was perfect. The music was in perfect timing. The songs and hymns had a beginning and an ending. Yet in heaven I was certain that time was stable, nothing dying or decaying, nothing hurried and nothing late.

Time seemed relaxed, comfortable, and natural. The limitations and consequences of earthly time did not apply here. Heavenly time and order were intertwined as part of the perfect whole.

I was outside the city, slowly moving toward its wall, suspended a few hundred feet above the ground. I'm not sure how I knew directions there, but I had a strong, almost magnetic sense, that it was northwest. Which meant I was approaching the city from the southeast.

A narrow road led to an entrance in the wall, which led into the city. I moved effortlessly along the road, escorted by my two angelic guides, on what seemed to be a divine schedule. Below me lay the purest, most perfect grass, precisely the right length and not a blade that was bent or even out of place. It was the most vibrant green I had ever seen. If a color can be said to be alive, the green I saw was alive, slightly transparent and emitting light and life from within each blade.

The iridescent grass stretched endlessly over gently rolling hills upon which were sprinkled the most colorful wild flowers, lifting their soft-petaled beauty skyward, almost as if they were a chorus of flowers caught up in their own way of praising God. The fragrance that permeated heaven was so gentle and sweet, I almost didn't notice it amid all there was to see and hear. But as I looked at the delicate, perfect flowers and grass, I wanted to smell them. Instantly, I was aware of a gentle aroma. As I focused, I could tell the difference between the grass and the flowers, the trees and even the air. It was all so pure and intoxicating and blended together in a sweet and satisfying scent.

In the distance stood a range of mountains, majestic in appearance, as if they reigned over the entire landscape. These were not mountains you wanted to conquer; these were mountains you wanted to revere.

It seemed that my vision had been extremely enhanced. How otherwise could I see the colors I was seeing or the light that was in everything? It was something like being in a 3-D movie and then putting on the 3-D glasses. Or being outside in the darkest night and putting on night goggles. Suddenly everything has more dimensions, more richness. But that is an understatement. Multiply that by ten thousand and it would be like what I was experiencing. There are no words that capture the scenes that were before me. Utterly breathtaking.

My body was elevated above the ground and moved effortlessly to whatever location my escorts determined. My energy seemed boundless, and even though I had always worked hard to be in excellent condition, I had never come close to feeling as strong and healthy as I felt now. It was as though I could accomplish anything.

The road was only wide enough for two people and followed the contours of the hills. Then it began sloping upward toward the huge wall that encircled the city. I gazed again at the light, which stunned me with its glorious brightness and drew me toward it. I wanted to take everything in, to see it all, absorb it all, and remember it all.

Next I heard the faint sound of water rushing in the distance. I couldn't see the water, but it sounded as if it were rivers cascading over a series of small waterfalls, creating music that was ever-changing.

Music was everywhere. The worship of God was the heart and focus of the music, and everywhere the joy of the music could be felt. The deepest part of my heart resonated with it, made me want to be a part of it forever. I never wanted it to stop. It swelled within me and without me as if it were inviting me into some divine dance.

The music was a seamless blend of vocals and instrumentals, the voices enhancing the instruments, and the instruments enhancing the vocals. Neither diminished the other but rather enriched the other. There was no competition, only cooperation. Perfect harmonic order. I had the feeling—and it was the most satisfying of feelings—that I was made for the music, as if each muscle in my body were a taut string of some finely tuned instrument, created to play the most beautiful music ever composed. I felt part of the music. One with it. Full of joy and wonder and worship. Perhaps this is what love sounds like when put to music. It felt so. And every part of me felt it.

I was in complete harmony with it, and it accompanied me, beguiling me onward throughout my journey. I thought I would burst with exuberance as I found myself included in such sacred and joyous melodies. I wanted to pause and let the music resonate so I could savor the glorious experience. But it never stopped. It just kept on playing.

The music of praise seemed to be alive and it passed through me, permeating every cell. My being seemed to vibrate like a divine tuning fork. I felt all this, every ecstatic moment of it. And I never wanted it to end. The music there, like the light that was there, existed in everything, and everything felt in perfect harmony. There was not a note of discord. Not a trace of someone playing his own music. Not a bit of competition anywhere. This was perfect unity. Expressed toward one focus—God.

It was as if all of heaven knew the beat, the tempo, the words, the pitch, the tone, and all participated in their unique way but in a way that all was united into one song. There were not different songs playing together; it was all one song, sung by everyone, simultaneously.

It was beautiful beyond belief. And it was blissful beyond belief. I never felt such overwhelming peace.

15

CELESTIAL PERFECTION

While in heaven, I somehow realized that knowledge is flawed and did not seem to be of great significance. Truth is what prevails and has supremacy in heaven. When I had questions or needed understanding it seemed to be imparted automatically and directly into my heart.

Just one of the things I somehow seemed to "understand" was that heavenly order was everywhere and in everything. I understood in my heart that God's will was perfection and His Word was the source of all creation. As I considered all that I had seen, I understood that the Word of God was and is the foundation for everything. God was the heart of heaven, His love, His will, His order.

Somehow I recognized that Jesus, the Word, was the structure that held it all together. Like the rib cage around the heart. He was the creative power that brought everything that I saw into place and stabilized it.

The multitudes of angels and people were responding to the will of God and acting in perfect order to accomplish His will. Even light—the way it traveled and reflected—was highly complex, yet mathematical and precise. The melodies and rhythms of the music were all in perfect order. Nothing out of sync. No part of heaven was independent of the whole. There was complete unity.

Between the central part of the city and the city walls were groupings of brightly colored picture-perfect homes in small, quaint towns. I'll call them townships, because I can't think of a better word for them. I focused on only three townships, but certainly there were more. A lot more, no doubt. The dwellings in these townships were not arranged in a uniform or symmetrical manner but appeared perfectly balanced somehow. Each home was customized and unique from the others yet blended harmoniously. Some were three or four stories, some were even higher. There were no two the same. If music could become homes, it would look like these, beautifully built and perfectly balanced.

The flowers in heaven fascinated me. Again, a delightful and delicate balance between diversity and unity. Each was unique. All were one. And they were beautiful to behold. Each petal and leaf illuminated with that glorious light and added just the right splashes of color to the velvety expanse of green grass.

As I described previously, the grass, the sky, the walls, the houses, everything was more beautiful than I ever dreamed anything could be. Even the colors. They were richer, deeper, more luminescent than any colors I have ever seen in the farthest reaches of earth or in the most fantastic of dreams. They were so vibrant they pulsated with life. Each and every color, no matter how varied, took its color from the glistening whiteness that permeated heaven.

If millions of jewels had been gathered into one place and the brightest sunlight shone through them, it wouldn't begin to describe the colors I saw. Heaven was filled with a rainbow of hues and provided me with a sensory feast.

My eyes were next drawn to a river that stretched from the gathering area in the middle of the city to the wall. It flowed toward the wall and seemed to end there, at least from my vantage point. The river was perfectly clear with a bluish-white hue. The light didn't shine on the water but mysteriously shone within it somehow.

The wall to the city was not a single wall but rather a series of walls layered next to each other. The wall was made of three outer layers, three inner layers, and one higher wall in the center. The outer layers of the wall were about forty feet tall. Each layer of the wall was taller as it got closer to the center, like a stairstep. At its tallest point the wall was a couple hundred feet. And surprisingly, it was as thick as it was tall. The wall was massive and stretched out to my left and right as far as I could see in both directions.

The outer wall was greenish in color with a hint of blue and a hint of black mingled within it. It was made entirely of translucent stones. Large multicolored stones were built into the base of the wall in layered rows. A powerful light permeated the wall, and you could see all the colors of the rainbow in it. Strangely, whenever I moved, the colors moved ever so slightly as if sensing my movement and making an adjustment.

The two angels that had escorted me there were still with me, moving me along, the three of us in sync, making sure I was *where* I should be, *when* I should be there.

I was eye-level with the base of the wall now and no longer hovering above it, but standing in front of an impressive opening. It was an archway that seemed to be approximately forty feet high and thirty to thirty-five feet wide.

A tall, majestic angelic being stood to the right side of the gate, dressed similarly to my escorts with the exception of the golden belt wrapped around his upper waist. A large emblem was located on the belt where a buckle would normally be. He appeared very strong and masculine. His hair was either white or it was the light radiating from him. But his entire being, and his head, specifically, was illuminated in bright white light. His face seemed to light up with love and joy at seeing me.

The entrance, or gateway, was opalescent in color, as if it had been made of pearls that had been liquefied, and then solidified onto the wall. The entrance was completely composed of this mesmerizing substance that also coated the entire inside of the opening as far as I could see. The ornamentation around the entrance included phenomenal detail. It was the most astounding sight I had ever seen. As I basked in the beauty that adorned the gateway, I noticed large gold letters emblazoned above the opening. They seemed to quiver with life. The single line of letters formed an arch over the entrance. I didn't recognize the letters but knew the words were as important as any words could be. Other letters were written in honey-colored gemstones on the ground in front of the entrance and included several lines. The entrance through the thick wall was breathtaking. The opening seemed filled with light that was the purest of white, yet it seemed to have countless hues that changed with even my slightest movement. I was filled with excited anticipation of entering that beautiful gate.

I was immersed in music, in light, and in love. Vibrant life permeated everything. All these weren't just *around* me, they were *inside* me. And it was wonderful, more wonderful than anything I had ever experienced. It felt as if I belonged there. I didn't want to leave. Ever. It was as if this was the place I had been searching all my life to find, and now I'd found it. My search was over!

A smaller group of people in soft-white robes had congregated to my left in the lush grass just off the roadway. It now seemed as if the music was orchestrating the event, moving people to their proper places. They had just arrived and were waiting in the wings, on time and in place, as if they followed a director's cue.

Who are these people? I wondered. *And why are they here?*

As suddenly as I had wondered, the answer came. They were here *for me*. Wherever they had traveled from and however far they had traveled, they had traveled *for me*. The looks on their faces, their excitement at seeing me, at welcoming me, was overwhelming. I felt so special, so loved. I had never felt such a deep sense of belonging. They radiated profound joy at seeing me. Everyone smiled, their eyes warm and kind; their hearts so filled with unconditional love that it spilled out of them onto me. No one was recognizable as an earthly acquaintance, but all seemed remarkably familiar. I didn't know these people, but somehow I knew they were my family—my spiritual family, my brothers, my sisters, spanning generations.

Although I didn't know them, somehow they knew me. They knew Dale Black. They knew my name. And they knew the *real* me, not the one I tried to project on earth to be accepted by someone I wanted to be friends with or to be validated by some group of peers I wanted to be part of.

They not only knew my name but somehow they knew the story behind my name. I was unaccustomed to such love and acceptance. I began to understand that this love is what God had designed for me from the beginning. These people had come to welcome me, include me, and communicate to me that I was a valuable part of the family of God. I had never felt so loved in my life, yet I had never done anything for these people. This was unconditional love. They were vessels of God's love. Both individually and collectively.

For some reason I clearly understood that I should not be touched, at least not yet. No one tried to touch me, and I didn't have a need to be embraced. The love I received from my spiritual family was so fulfilling and satisfying that no human touch could rival how loved I felt.

As I gazed into the radiant faces of these precious people, I looked into eyes that were more colorful than any on earth. Their smiles were brighter. Their countenances more alive. Each person was a living, vibrant, eternal being, exuding the very life of God.

I didn't think about whether they were male or female, although there were both. I saw them for who they were. None were skinny, none overweight. None were crippled, none were bent or broken. None were old, none were young. If I had to guess, I would say they appeared to be somewhere around thirty years old. They had no wrinkles, no signs of shifting or sagging, no signs of aging at all. I somehow understood that time was not an enemy here. Although some form of time does seem to exist in heaven, no one aged. No one died. Nothing decayed.

They wore soft-white seamless robes. Their skin tones were different but blended together so that no single person stood out. I did not notice racial differences, but I was aware that they had come from many tribes and nations.

None were recognized by the physical or social distinctions that we recognize on earth. All were recognized by their spirit, by the essence of who they were. Everyone and everything was full of pure life and was connected to the light somehow, and everything that was connected led to God.

Part of the joy I was experiencing was not only the presence of everything wonderful but the absence of everything terrible. There was no strife, no competition, no sarcasm, no betrayal, no deception, no lies, no murders, no unfaithfulness, no disloyalty, nothing contrary to the light and life and love.

In short, there was no sin.

And the absence of sin was something you could feel. There was no shame, because there was nothing to be ashamed of. There was no sadness, because there was nothing to be sad about. There was no need to hide, because there was nothing to hide from. It was all out in the open. Clean and pure.

Here was perfection. Complete and utter perfection. The revelation of sin's absence was astounding and exhilarating. This is where I belonged. I was made to be in heaven. In a perfect place where there is no sin.

I had been in heaven for some time before I recognized sin's absence. Now I contemplated the one thing that *dominated everything* on earth … that *infected everything* on earth, but was missing here. It can be compared to oxygen. I went through life not really thinking about the air I was breathing while I worked, slept, ate, and drove. But take that air away and I would think about nothing else. Similarly, I was so accustomed to sin that I hadn't even recognized its far-reaching effects in every part of life. But nothing had been tainted in heaven by sin's destructive touch. This perfection I experienced was largely due to the absence of sin.

The best unity I have ever felt on earth did not compare with the exhilarating oneness that I experienced with my spiritual family in heaven. This love … God's love, was transforming. To experience something so sacred, so profound as the boundless love of God was the most thrilling part of heaven. It satisfied a longing in the deepest part of me. My spiritual family had shared God's perfect love with me. How could I ever be the same?

My attention was diverted to the beautiful entrance. I was certain I was going through the gate. Again I turned back toward my precious family and did not want to leave that perfect love. But because of the highly expectant look on their smiling faces, it seemed as if they knew I would be given a gift and what that gift would do for me.

I felt so special, you can't believe how special. After all, all this was *for me*. Everyone there was there *for me*. I had no idea what gift I was to receive, but the anticipation on the faces of the people let me know that it was something extraordinary.

I felt like a kid again, like that fifth-grade kid who loved God. Like that kid who used to look forward to Christmas like you wouldn't believe. I couldn't wait to open the gifts that waited for me under the tree. And I couldn't wait for the gift that waited for me now.

The music continued, such beautiful music, and I became even more excited. It swelled and with it so did my anticipation.

And then, as I was about to travel through the entrance and receive the gift . . .

I was swept away.

(16)

ASK AND RECEIVE

It was springtime, and I was back for yet another visit with Dr. Graham. This time I brought flowers for his receptionist.

"Oh, Dale! What a surprise!"

"It's the least I can do for all you have done for me."

"Well, it's no secret that you are our favorite patient." She winked and lowered her voice. "Even Doc has a special place in his heart for you, Dale. But, of course, he'll never let *you* know."

My weekly checkups had grown into pleasant afternoon diversions. I felt such gratitude for Dr. Graham's staff. They were so caring, so loving. The quiet, reserved concern of the doctor touched me even more.

This particular day I was feeling on top of the world. After the routine X rays and exam, the doctor simply said, "Dale, I'd like to meet with you in my office next week." His face was as inscrutable as ever.

"Great! See you next week, Doc!"

He left the room, and I picked up my crutches and walked down the hall, where I went past autographed photographs of Evel Knievel, Peggy Fleming, and dozens of other sports figures and television celebrities.

All the way down the hall I wondered what he wanted to see me about, why he didn't say more. I couldn't imagine what it might be. Nothing serious, surely. After all, I was out of the woods on all the serious stuff.

The following week I returned with new gifts in hand. After the X rays, which he normally went over with me in the examination room, he took me to his private office. The stuffed chair was stiff, and I felt even stiffer. He sat at his desk, quietly looking over my file as I fidgeted in anticipation.

"OK, Dale. I've got good news and bad news."

"Where have I heard that before?" A big smile stretched across my face and pulled painfully at my stitches.

"Your shoulder is doing well," he said matter-of-factly. "Have you been exercising it?"

I chuckled. "I guess you can call it that. I call it T-A-S . . . training in aeronautical sciences! When I'm driving my car, I stick my arm out the window and let the wind lift it. I can't move it on my own yet, but depending on the angle of my hand, I get quite a bit of elevated movement and stretching from the wind. I know it's making the shoulder stronger."

He cracked his first smile. "You're right. It is getting stronger. In fact, your shoulder is the most amazing thing I've seen in my medical career."

"I'm guessing that's not the reason you wanted to meet with me."

"No. The reason is your ankle."

"My ankle? I thought it was healing just fine."

"When we observed the blood beginning to circulate in your ankle, I really believed that your faith played a part in that. Regrettably, the blood supply hasn't increased beyond the 15 percent I observed when we examined it last."

He paused, as if trying to find the right words. But no words came.

"What do you recommend?" I asked.

He got up from his desk and pulled a thick leather-bound medical book off the shelf, opening it to a page he had marked. He looked at the page, then at me.

"I believe we need to operate on your ankle immediately. There is no time to lose. We need to perform a bone fusion, removing pieces of the bone from your hip and attaching them to your leg and foot bones. This will result in permanent immobility of the ankle, but it will allow you to at least put weight on it in the future."

His finger conspicuously tapped at a picture in the medical book. I don't know what I said next. But I knew I needed time to process what Dr. Graham had said.

It was a big decision. A permanent decision.

I left the office quickly, without small-talking with the receptionist or the usual chorus of good-byes to the staff.

My plans that afternoon included another flight with Capt. Fred Griffith, the test pilot who had flown me over the monument for the first time after the crash. He was going to take me flying again. I was more prepared for it this time, both emotionally and physically... until my visit with Dr. Graham. His news knocked the wind out of me. The last thing I felt like was getting into a plane, a plane I would never again fly if I had the operation that Dr. Graham felt was so critical.

I was confused and angry. I pulled my car over to use a pay phone and canceled the flight with Fred. I drove and drove and drove, trying to get it out of my system. *How could God do this? I mean, good grief, what does He want from me? I've sought Him. I've taken care of myself, followed the doctor's orders. I've shared His love with others. I believed God's Word, believed He would heal me. Now this.*

I caught the Ventura Freeway, wound around the interchange, and drove south to Long Beach. I needed a second opinion.

I respected my grandpa enormously. As I closed the door to his office, I hadn't even sat down before the news spilled out of me. I repeated what Dr. Graham had said.

Fusion is permanent. And permanent is a long time. If I got the ankle fused, walking would be difficult, sports would be something I watched on TV, and flying...

Forget flying.

Forever.

One question seemed paramount. *Why?*

Grandpa leaned forward, looking directly into my eyes. "Dale, you receive healing by faith, not by sight!" Those were Grandpa's first words. "It's not what you see on the X-ray machine that matters. What matters is what God says about it and then what you're going to believe in your heart."

Grandpa and I continued our discussion as I wiped the stream of tears from my eyes.

"Dale, the Bible says in Hebrews the eleventh chapter, that 'faith is the substance of things hoped for, the evidence of things not seen.' That means that what you see, feel, or hear isn't the final word. Don't be moved by your physical senses or the circumstances around you. I'm not saying to ignore what the doctors say. Not at all. They are professionals, and they are here to help, and God uses doctors in mighty ways. But above all else, when push comes to shove, believe what God has said. Do what God's Word says to do. Do what you believe in your heart God is telling you to do."

I stared blankly at the tough, stubborn man of faith who sat across from me. His face was flushed with the intensity of his words. Yet I simply could not grasp the full impact of all that he was saying. I still didn't know if God wanted me to have the surgery.

At last, in a burst of frustration, I said, "Look, Grandpa. I'm going to take this piece of paper." I ripped a sheet off a legal pad that he'd placed next to his open Bible. "I'm gonna write down everything you say. . . ."

"Dale, don't put your faith in me. That will never work. Eventually all men will fail. But God cannot fail. And it is impossible for God to lie. Dale, your faith must be in God and in His Word." His voice was kind but firm.

I responded, "No, don't worry, Gramps. I'm not putting my faith in you, it's just that you've been a DOER of God's Word a lot longer than I have, and I know you can help direct me to the right principles in the Bible. But I will guarantee you this: Whatever I write on this list, I am going to do. After I have done everything that I write down, then all I have to do is wait on God."

"OK, Dale, you work that out between God and yourself. But here is what I recommend for you because this has been my experience." And so Grandpa began to list the principles he had learned while seeking the will of God.

"First of all, pray. Pray alone, pray with the elders, and pray with your friends. Just make sure that your prayer partners really believe and agree with you that God *will* answer your prayer."

I carefully wrote down everything on my checklist. Pray. Pray alone and in a group of only those who believe.

"Second, Dale, read your Bible."

I interrupted. "Read what? Where do I begin?"

"Let God show you, Dale; just start reading," Grandpa replied. "Something in the Bible will jump out at you as if it were printed in big red letters. God will have special chapters and verses for you. Special words will speak directly to your heart. He will lead you to them if you will ask and then expect Him to lead."

Being a young, underdeveloped Christian, I thought this all sounded pretty mysterious. "But I am going to do every last thing on this list. I refuse to be a hearer only! I will become a doer of God's Word!"

Grandpa hesitated for a moment, then continued. "Third, Dale, do exactly what God says in the Bible. Be on guard and ready, however, because in my experience I've learned that your faith will be tested in order to be strengthened. Understand, it is not God testing your faith, but He is allowing it to be tested to determine whether you really believe in your heart what God has promised. And remember, Dale, God's will is what you're looking for, and His will is found in His Word. He will never violate His Word."

Grandpa's words burned into my heart, and I was sure that I would never forget a single thing he had said. Nevertheless, I carefully folded the piece of paper with my checklist on it and tucked it securely into my shirt pocket, determined to follow each bit of instruction to the letter.

Now that I had discussed my fears and hopes about my ankle with Grandpa and had a plan to follow, I needed to talk to him about another equally difficult subject. I shifted in my chair, adjusted my cast and braces, trying to find a comfortable position. He leaned forward, peered deep into my eyes, and asked, "What else is troubling you, Dale?"

I had spent a lot of time with my grandfather. We were very close, and I knew my grandfather loved me. He communicated his love by listening well and giving me his time when I needed it.

Russell Price commanded a great deal of respect among his peers and was known by all as a man of principle who possessed a strong backbone. He was a man of his word. He lived in a world governed by principles. The most important things in his life were God, his family, his church, and his business . . . in that order.

Of course I loved Grandpa, and respected him too. That's why I found myself in his office that spring afternoon. I now told him about the returning memories of the crash. Next, I nervously confessed to him that I had observed my body on the operating table. Timidly I began to share vivid memories of heaven but only in a brief, general way. First I wanted to "test the waters" to see how he'd react. I briefly explained the wall, the people, the music, but did not go into much detail.

"Dale, before you go on, may I say a few things?" he asked.

I nodded. "Sure, of course, that's exactly why I'm here."

"In my lifetime, Dale, I've observed many people before you who have used supernatural experiences to gain accolades from others. Many books have been written about this, and these people go around the country speaking on the subject to fan the flame of self-promotion. But in my opinion, most of this is done for financial gain or recognition and is not pleasing to the Lord. Dale, when you're dealing with things like heaven and eternity, you're operating in God's realm. That realm is the spiritual, and I think you need to be cautious. If God has truly given you these experiences, then those experiences are sacred, aren't they?"

I looked into his well-wrinkled, warm, and kind face but didn't say a word.

"Dale," he continued, "I don't hesitate for a second to believe that the experiences you have now remembered are real. I've known you all your life and I know your heart. If God has allowed you to see a glimpse of heaven, even if you were in heaven for a time, then you have a couple of options. You can speak about your experience, or you can treat the experience as sacred and let your life be a reflection of your experience. By that I mean, if you really did see the other side, then live out whatever you believe you saw. Live what you believe you heard. Just live what you learned. Your life's actions will speak louder than your voice."

Moments passed and neither of us said a word. He was giving me time to think and process.

Finally, my grandfather muttered while staring out his office window, "That might explain why you had no internal injuries or major brain damage." He wiped tears from his eyes and said, "Well, praise the Lord."

I had asked Grandpa specific questions hundreds of times before and was always glad that I had. I decided to ask another one. "Grandpa, what would you do if you were in my shoes?"

"Dale, let me say, if it were me, I would not use the experience for personal gain. Look, I'm not faulting others, and I'm not judging what others do. But you asked me my opinion, and I'm giving it to you. Live what you saw, Dale. Live what you believe you've learned from those experiences. I wouldn't go around telling anyone anything until God has specifically instructed you to. If your experience in heaven was real, then let your life say so. And if the experiences were really from God, they will not go away. They will become a permanent part of you.

"You can do what you want with this, Dale, and I'll not judge you one way or the other. You can write about it, speak about it, or you can quietly live it instead. It's totally up to you. But make sure that you hear from God. Spend enough time in prayer to know what He's telling you to do."

Of course, none of what Grandpa shared surprised me; I knew him well. Finally, I thanked him for taking the time and hobbled out of his office.

As I drove home, I began to talk to God. I felt as if He were right there with me. My problem was His problem.

"Lord," I prayed as I drove. "You made the world. You made the stars and everything in the universe. You created everything in existence." I paused and unconsciously held my breath. I felt as if God had just shown me how the power of His spoken Word created all things in existence. It seemed to suddenly all make sense.

"O God, You are so completely awesome!" I pondered these thoughts as I made my way southbound on the 405 bound for the Seal Beach Boulevard off-ramp. "And God, You made my ankle too. You know exactly what is wrong with it and how to fix it again. Father, I've read in the Bible that Jesus healed everyone that asked. He didn't turn anyone down. It seems clear to me, Lord, that the Bible indicates that healing is available to everyone. Therefore, I believe it is Your will to heal me too. I believe without doubt that You want me healed and that You want to restore my ankle."

After parking my MGB, wanting to give the raw skin under my arms a needed reprieve from the constant use of crutches, I hopped on my right leg into the house. Without a moment's hesitation, I made my way to my room and picked up my Bible. I held it in my hands for a few minutes, wondering where to turn and what to read.

"God, You have something special to say to me through Your Word, right?" I held the Bible in both hands. "Lord! Please tell me where to read. Where should I begin?"

I waited for a moment. Suddenly the number *seven,* then Matthew, chapter 7, entered my mind as if it were a photograph. At first I assumed this was just my imagination. But the mental picture could not be erased. Matthew, chapter 7, persisted.

Somewhat skeptically, I turned the pages until I found the seventh chapter of Matthew: *"Judge not, that you be not judged. For with what judgment you judge, you will be judged. . . ."* As I read, I thought, W*hat does this have to do with my ankle?*

Verse by verse I read on. And then it happened, just like Grandpa had said it would. My eyes were fixed on the verse, and the words leapt out at me as if they had my name printed all over them. The words seemed to grab me by the neck and shake me.

Matthew 7:7–8, *"Ask, and it will be given to you; seek, and you will find; knock, and it will be opened to you. For everyone who asks receives, and he who seeks finds, and to him who knocks it will be opened."*

God had led me to this simple statement of faith that had challenged His people for centuries. Was I any less likely to receive or find or enter into His dwelling place than any other of His children?

Then I said, "God, You said that everyone who asks, receives, and he who seeks, finds. God, that means me! And I ask You right now to heal my ankle so I can walk and run someday. Thank You, God. I believe You are answering this prayer even now."

The decision was made, then and there. "Lord, I am making a choice. I'm deciding to believe that You are going to answer my prayers and heal my ankle. I am asking You to do what is impossible in the natural realm.

"God, if I'm ever going to walk again, if I'm ever going to play sports again..." By now tears were streaming down my face. I could barely see, but my prayer poured out like a river. "God, if I'm ever going to fly again..." I choked in my emotion. "Lord, if I am ever going to walk or play sports or fly, it will be for one reason. That reason will be that You healed me according to Your Word. I trust You, Lord, and I believe in You and Your Word! And I'll be careful to give You the glory."

I stood up as if to deliver the final verdict. "God, I believe that it is not Your will for me to have this bone fusion operation! I respect Dr. Graham and I appreciate him, but You will be the one to perform this operation in Your way. And with You as my Physician, I will have normal use of my ankle someday."

"Thank You, God ... thank You, Father," I whispered, wiping my eyes. With that, I closed my Bible. From that moment on, the course was set ... the flight plan was filed. Under His wings I would be carried to the destination of His choosing.

Over the next few days, I confirmed another decision in my mind and settled it in my heart. I would live what I learned from my experiences in heaven. I decided not to share my sacred experiences with anyone—not my parents, not my girlfriend, not even my wife or children, should I ever have them. Until God clearly instructed me otherwise, these experiences would be kept between Him and me alone. And I knew Gramps would keep my secret. I asked God for the strength to live a life that would reflect the experiences He blessed me with. I would need His power and strength to bring glory to Him by becoming that reflection of His faith, hope, and love.

The next day I phoned Grandpa. He seemed pleased to hear my decision but reminded me not to get my eyes off God's Word and His promise. Then I phoned Dr. Graham. That was entirely another story.

"Dale, you're making a mistake, a *serious* mistake. You are gambling with your ability to walk again, to *ever* walk again. If the circulation in your ankle doesn't improve, you won't be able to move it, let alone put any weight on it. Your ankle will collapse. Arthritis will set in. And you will be in severe pain the rest of your life. With no cure. Am I making myself clear? Do you understand, Dale?"

The words were hard to hear. The tone was even harder. I told him how much I respected him, how much I appreciated all he had done for me, but my decision was final.

I believed God was going to let me fly again. If I was ever to do that, it wouldn't be with a fused ankle. I made the decision in faith. I'm sure Dr. Graham thought I had made it in presumption. Regardless, I was the one who had to live with the consequences.

✈

"Hello, Mrs. Ferguson? This is Dale Black." I felt a little foolish making the call, but I was determined to do it anyway. "In James, the fifth chapter, the Bible instructs us to call for the elders of the church and have them pray, if any is sick. I wanted to ask you and your husband to pray about something for me."

She didn't hesitate at all. "Sure, Dale. What is it?"

I read from the scribbled notes I'd made on the paper in Gramps' office.

"Well, it's about some things that I'm asking God to do in my body. He started a miracle in my ankle, but then it seemed as if He quit! But now I believe He is going to restore my ankle all the way, 100 percent. I need some believers to pray in agreement with me. Would you pray for me and specifically ask God to restore blood circulation in my left ankle?"

Grandpa had specifically said to make sure that those I asked to pray truly believed that God would do what He says. I knew that the Fergusons and my uncle and aunt, Jerry and Verna Price, would be the ones to ask for prayers of faith. They sincerely loved me, but, more important, they had faith in an all-powerful God who desires to heal and answer prayer.

After speaking to them, I went outside to catch some fresh late-afternoon air. There stood a familiar smiling face. It was our friendly next-door neighbor, young Terry Smith. Terry's father was a retired airline pilot. "How are you getting along, Dale?"

Here was my first opportunity to speak about my faith in God's Word regarding my ankle. "Well, Terry, I'm getting along great! God is completely healing my ankle. He's producing another miracle in my body, and I'm very grateful. And Terry, how's it going with you?"

Within two hours of reading the seventh chapter of Matthew, I had made a decision not to have the operation of fusing bone from my hip into my ankle. Four people were now praying in faith for my ankle to be restored. Yet I began to realize the first person that needed to be convinced that God's Word was true in my life was the one looking back in the mirror—me. I didn't completely understand it all at first. But as I repeated promises from the Bible and spoke out loud about those words to myself and to others, something wonderful was happening. Those Bible promises began to take root in my heart.

"Now faith is the substance of things hoped for," I reminded myself, "the evidence of things not seen." Evidence—that's the kind of hard facts lawyers present that must stand up in a court of law. I was beginning to understand.

There was a kind of exhilaration to this new experiment in obedience to God's Word. I felt as if I were beginning an adventure with the God who created me. And that's exactly what it was. He and I were going to travel together. He would instruct; I would obey and learn.

Because of my inexperience, though, I had not counted on discouraging words, disappointing circumstances, or devastating medical reports. My first unexpected detour came when my father heard that I had decided not to have the bone-fusion surgery recommended by Dr. Graham. "Dale, I think you're being unrealistic," he said.

It was difficult to disagree with my dad. He was a strong individual and a successful businessman, president of his own company, one of the spin-offs of the family business. He had also seen me through the entire airplane crash ordeal, and he had shared my burden without complaint. It was Dad and Grandpa who had believed that prayer would heal my ankle in the first place. On my behalf they rejected one operation just after the crash and their decision turned out to be the best one for me. But now I felt sad saying, "No, Dad, I've made up my mind. I've already asked God to heal my ankle, and I'm going to believe that He will."

When I returned to the college campus, I had dozens of opportunities to verbally confirm my newfound perspective.

When friends asked how I was doing, I had a standard reply: "God has healed me. Praise the Lord! Soon I'll have new X rays to prove it! You watch. You wait. You'll see."

As the time of my next doctor's appointment came around, I gathered up five friends who wanted to see the miracle firsthand. We piled into an old green Cadillac and headed for Burbank. As we drove, I reminded them of our purpose: "You guys are going to be eyewitnesses to an awesome miracle."

We cruised happily along the freeway, parked, then descended upon the medical building like a small, loyal regiment of soldiers. We were full of youthful zeal. Dr. Graham's staff, somewhat used to my eccentric behavior, graciously welcomed my friends.

"They're here to see that God has healed my ankle," I explained.

The X rays were taken. We waited anxiously until Dr. Graham emerged with them in hand. "Wait, Doc. Before you put up the X rays, would you mind if we prayed together and thanked God for what He has already done?"

Doctor Graham nodded OK to my request. The six of us held hands as we gathered around the viewing screen to pray. We thanked the Lord for what He had done and for what we were about to see. After we said amen, Dr. Graham placed the negatives on the screen to begin his analysis.

He paused a long time before he spoke. At last, and with some difficulty, he broke the news. "There is absolutely no progress. I'm sorry, Dale, the blood is not circulating in your ankle."

Even though the war was far from being over, that little battle marked a heavy defeat. My friends and I were an untrained unit. Our equipment and weapons had not been previously tested. As for me, I was only beginning to learn how to put on the full armor of God. I had a long, long way to go.

Subdued and thoughtful, we headed back to the car. "Don't worry, Dale, God is certainly not finished yet!" Dave patted me on the back as he spoke. Gene, Larry, Jerry, and others offered their own guarded condolences.

I told my friends that I didn't want to talk. I turned and gazed out the window, discouraging further communication. It was uncomfortable for everyone anyway. And it was a good thing, because inside I was becoming self-centered again. In my heart, thoughts that I was ashamed of exposed themselves. *Don't give me all those neat little answers and clichés. It's my life, not yours. You have no idea how I feel!* The cold fact was this: *God did not do what He told me He would do. God let me down. He blew it and I don't like it at all! I have acted like a fool by trusting Him!* My thoughts riveted to the possibility that maybe Dr. Graham was right. Maybe I had made a choice that would leave me more crippled than I had dared believe. Was God that unfair? Was He that hard to figure out? What was I going to do now?

All at once I remembered—the checklist! Had God allowed my faith to be tested? I recalled Grandpa Price cautioning me that once my faith was put into action, I would be tested back. I had told hundreds of people that my ankle was healed. I wasn't playing games. I had truly believed it to be so. But what had happened? When the X rays came back with a negative report, I had believed them more than God's Word. I listened to the wrong voice. I believed in circumstances and let go of the promise of God! How could I have let it happen?

My faith grew as I studied the Bible and replaced my doubt with increasing faith in the promises of God.

Within days I was standing in the college chapel service, giving my testimony again. I shared my renewed faith in God's Word, and the importance of patience and long-suffering with faith in prayer. After sharing my experience, Rev. Reuben Welch anointed me with oil and prayed for me while others prayed for the bones in my ankle to be restored.

I invited any who were interested to return the next morning to Dr. Graham's office for another opportunity to see a miracle. I explained to them that my faith had been put to the test. "Come and see the miracle!" I announced to the students in the chapel. This time, the well-worn green Cadillac and a second car made their way to Burbank, loaded with high-strung Christian students who believed in a miracle-working God.

Before our group got out of the car, we had a word of prayer and thanked God for what He had already done. The last episode had been a test of my faith. I had clearly flunked. But now I knew where I had made my mistake. Most people have heard the phrase "seeing is believing." But according to the Bible I had now learned that "believing is seeing." Now was the time for what I believed would become something we could all see.

I thought I finally understood. I was certain I had uncovered the keys to finding the will of God—by *knowing* the promises in the Word of God. Little did I know that the most important lessons about God and His will lay just ahead of me. What I was to learn about myself in the process would not only surprise me but would change me forever.

"Now faith is the substance of things hoped for, the evidence of things not seen."—Hebrews 11:1

(17)

LOSING LIFE TO FIND IT

Once again in Dr. Graham's office, we went through the same procedures. The X rays were taken, and as before, we gathered around the viewing screen. I explained to the doctor briefly what had gone wrong the last time. I told him how I had failed to realize that my faith must be in the promises of God and not in circumstances. We held hands and prayed, thanking God for His love and for His Word.

Dr. Graham placed the negatives on the screen. On this occasion, it took the long-suffering doctor even longer to speak.

Finally, he turned to me and revealed his findings. "Dale, I'm sorry." He was clearly struggling. "Not only is there no progress, but now we have waited too long. There is no blood circulation in your ankle. There is nothing we can do to reverse the situation. The bone is completely dead."

I was stunned. How could this be? I had done what I was supposed to do. I had corrected my error. This was not the way things were supposed to work. I had followed the checklist perfectly. My thoughts and questions could not be contained. As far as I was concerned, the news was as bad as it could be, and I was devastated. If I could not trust God, then I could never trust anyone or anything. Ever.

As we made our way back toward campus, no one said a word. I wanted it quiet and everyone knew it. After an hour of tense silence in the car, we finally arrived back on campus. No one was more relieved than I was. I hurried as quickly as my crutches could carry me to my dorm room, where

I shut and locked the door. I didn't want to see anyone. I was assaulted with such immense, overwhelming doubts and fears that I crumbled beneath them. *You're a fool, Dale Black. You're a stupid fool to put your complete trust in God. You obviously don't know what you're doing, and now you'll never walk again. You can forget about sports. Flying is out of the question, forever. All because of your idiotic faith experiment. God doesn't heal everybody. You can't make the decision to have God heal you. It was a big mistake not to have had that bone fusion operation. At least you could have walked again. But no, you had to act like some big man of faith. Welcome to the world of lifetime cripples. How could you be so foolish? Now you've lost everything, Dale.*

It was extremely difficult for me to sit comfortably. I didn't like to lie down because of my various casts and braces. But it also hurt to sit upright for very long. The most practical place for me to spend any amount of time was on my knees. The next day that's exactly where I found myself, on my knees at the side of my bed. Desperate. And alone.

I had locked the door because there wasn't a person on the face of the earth that I wanted to talk to. I only wanted to talk to God, but what I had to say was not particularly reverent. "God, You have blown it! I have made an absolute fool of myself in front of the medical staff and in front of my friends. Not only that, but we've made a real mess of making my life into one that gives You glory. Worst of all, my vocational goals have come to a dead end. I am crippled for life. Severe arthritis is just around the corner."

What I was saying was incorrect and I knew it, but I continued anyway. "Why didn't You do what You said You would do in those promises from the Bible? Are You playing some kind of game with me? I did everything on the list, right? I did everything. But You didn't keep Your part of the bargain, God. Could You explain why? What else do You want from me? Do You really want me in a wheelchair for life? Is that it? Well that's exactly what You've got!"

After I finished my selfish temper tantrum, I heard a clear yet gentle voice in my heart. In the exhausted quietness of my spirit, I sensed the tender voice of God's Spirit. "Dale, why do you want to be healed so badly? *'Seek first the kingdom of God, and His righteousness, and all these things will be added to you.'"*

I had read that Scripture recently, several times, but somehow I had just passed by the part about "His righteousness." Now tears began to flow down my face and once more I sensed Him speaking to me. "Seek Me first. And My righteousness, Dale. And all these things will be added to you."

I knew exactly what He meant. I should have been seeking the Healer before the healing. I wanted a miracle more than I wanted the Miracle Worker. And His other words rang in my spiritual ears. "*His* righteousness... *His* righteousness."

Despite my outspoken faith, despite my Christian words, despite my best efforts, I knew very well that I was not leading a completely pure life. There were still hidden sins in my life that I didn't want to deal with. My stubborn demands for a miracle were right at the top of the list. I knew that the answer to my prayers would glorify God, but I was really more interested in what it would do for me.

In those moments, everything changed. I finally gave up *all*. I surrendered *all* my life to God. I invited Him into every part of my life and asked Him to take complete control. "Lord, I'm so sorry. I'm living on borrowed time anyway. Every day of life is a gift from You. It is so obvious to everyone, especially me, that Dale Black should have died in that plane crash. I have nothing to lose, wheelchair or not."

If I've seen heaven, why am I still so self-centered? I couldn't understand it. I fell before the Lord and just wept.

I wept as if my tears could wash away all the dreams I had treasured for a unique, adventurous life. "I give up my obsession to walk again. I give up flying, sports, my quest for respect from others, everything. Lord, it's up to You. I will still pray for healing because I believe that is what Your will is for me according to Your Word. But this time I'll put You first in my life. First place in my dreams."

Then and there I decided that no matter what the cost, I would serve Him. I gave up my selfish goals and plans. "God, if You can use me better as a twenty-year-old in a wheelchair, as a cripple, then not my will but Yours be done."

At that moment I experienced something that had never happened to me before in my young life. I had a physical sensation that felt as if a heavy, rich substance, like oil, was being poured upon my head and was flowing over every part of me. The feeling was overwhelming and unforgettable. I was filled with joy and peace, and I felt completely free!

Within a few days I was asked to share once again in the Wednesday night chapel service. I shared a very simple message about submitting to God in every area of our lives. I didn't mention my ankle—or anything about me, for that matter. My conversations with everyone changed from talk of miracles on the outside to talk of a broken will and submitted heart on the inside.

When it came time for my next appointment with Dr. Graham, I did not invite anyone to join me. Instead, I went alone.

It had been two weeks since I had surrendered my entire will to God. Two weeks since I had felt the warm "oil" upon me. Two weeks since I had resigned myself to a life in a wheelchair, if that was what God wanted for me.

On the way to the doctor's appointment my car found its way to the familiar Valhalla Memorial Park, and I pulled over and stopped just a few feet from the Portal of the Folded Wings. On countless occasions since the crash I had spent time there with God. There I asked Him questions. There I reviewed in my mind the sequence of the aircraft smashing into the monument and my body falling to the ground. There at the monument I again sat in wonder of what He had done in sparing my life.

On this day I reviewed the checklist of the previous months. But this time I renewed my love for God and vowed to serve Him for the remainder of my days. The borrowed old green Cadillac then weaved through traffic along the familiar trek to Dr. Graham's office.

I quietly entered the doctor's waiting room. I whispered a prayer in my heart: *I give myself to You, God.* I had no expectations. Just a desire to be all that God wanted me to be.

After a review of all my injuries, Dr. Graham took the normal X rays of my ankle. He placed them up on the viewing screen to look at them. His voice was strangely soft and characteristically monotone. "Your ankle is healing, Dale. The blood has started circulating again." He paused as he pointed to the screen. "I don't understand it." His focus dropped to the floor as he shook his head in wonder. "I cannot tell you why, Dale, but your ankle has healed more in the past two weeks than it has in the entire past six months combined."

He lifted his eyes to look into my face as if he might find the answer there. Then he shook his head one last time. "I don't understand it at all. . . ."

In the quietness of that moment, deep within my spirit, there was a resounding echo, *"He who loses his life for My sake will find it."*

18

ON WINGS LIKE EAGLES

It was a long, hard spring. I had dropped out of Pasadena College after six grueling weeks. I pushed my body too hard, and it pushed back, refusing the rigorous schedule I was putting it through.

As the sap returned to the trees and their branches began to bud, I felt my body was going through a springtime of its own. One by one, the bandages came off. The stitches. The wires. I was down to one cast. The one on my left leg and ankle.

I continued ground-training classes at the junior college. And I continued flying lessons.

I also started working out at the gym. All my muscles had atrophied, but I couldn't do anything about that until my bones healed. The progress was slow. I did curls with my right arm, and gradually the strength came back. My left arm was another story. I was able to raise it to about a 45-degree angle, but it took a lot of effort and the pain was excruciating.

That was all the encouragement I needed. I hit the gym that much harder, hit the books that much harder, hit everything harder and faster.

Now that the vertebrae in my back had mended, I was doing sit-ups. I was wearing my patch on my good eye, forcing me to work the muscles in the injured eye.

Two weeks before the anniversary date of the crash, the cast came off. The leg looked like a toothpick, the foot was shriveled up, and the ankle, well, it looked pathetic.

But I was determined to make that date with the monument, and I worked hard, pushing myself through the pain. The back pain. The shoulder pain. The ankle pain.

As it turned out, I had pushed too hard.

The closer I got to the anniversary of the crash, the more the ankle swelled. And the more it swelled, the more painful it became, until I could hardly walk. I was trying so hard to do everything I could to get my body ready for the anniversary flight. I had promised myself and anyone who would listen that I would fly again over the monument as pilot in command. Now it was just days away. Even though my body was making amazing progress, it would take a miracle to pass an FAA medical in time to keep that date.

FRIDAY, JULY 17, 1970

The day before the anniversary of my crash.

No way. Who am I kidding? Me? Getting in a plane and flying over the crash site?

Tomorrow I'll look like a fool. A braggart full of myself. What was I thinking?

I'm not a teenager any longer. I'm twenty years old. I should know better. I should have listened to the doctor. I should have—

Incriminating thoughts cornered me, wagging their accusatory fingers.

Who do you think you are?

The problem isn't the swelling in your ankle; it's the swelling in your head.

I looked at the mirror. The patch mocked me. I took off my clothes, getting ready for bed. My right arm looked like it belonged to a Titan; the left arm, to a wimp. I tried to raise it. The pain was excruciating. I managed to lift it to about a 60-degree angle from my body, but only for a second and it took every ounce of strength I had.

I looked down at my legs. My right one looked like it was chiseled from a quarry; my left one, gimpy and discolored. I followed the grotesque sight down to my ankle. It was the size of a large grapefruit.

The ankle that refused to die!

I might be able to squeak my arm past the medical examiner, but not this. It would look as though I were trying to smuggle some kind of contraband fruit past customs.

Stripped not only of my clothes but also of any selfish pride, I knelt beside the bed. Like I had done so many times before, I bowed my head and prayed out loud a child's prayer.

"Lord, tomorrow is the anniversary of the plane crash, July 18. It's been a whole year. I am in such better shape than I was just after the crash last year. Better physically. Better spiritually. More than anyone could have dreamed. I praise You for that. I thank You for that. And I give You the glory."

I paused, wondering what the next thought should be, wondering if I could even put it into words.

"God, so many times in the Bible I've read about the way You speak to people in dreams."

And I felt awkward asking this, the way a child feels awkward about asking for something that's not his but that he wants really, really bad.

"Would You give me a special dream tonight? Talk to me, please? Tell me . . . whatever You want to tell me, OK?"

Again I paused, like a kid collecting his thoughts, then, with his arms full, realizing he has forgotten one.

"Oh, and Father, I promised a lot of people that I would fly over the air memorial as pilot in command on the first anniversary. It's not humanly possible, I know that. I can see that. My ankle would have to be almost normal to pass the exam. And I would have to convince someone to allow me to rent their aircraft. And fly by myself. On crutches and all. God, this would require a couple more miracles from You. And all within twelve hours. But Lord, if this would bring glory to You, or if for some other reason You want this to happen . . . please work it out."

Then I prayed something uncharacteristic of me, something Jesus prayed in the garden of Gethsemane; and in doing so, I exchanged more of my self-will for surrender.

"I would sure like to fly tomorrow, if You would allow it. But Your will be done, not mine."

A peace I can't describe came over me.

"Father, thanks for life. Thanks for Your unending love."

I took a deep breath, not quite sure how to end. Feeling a little clumsy with my words, but also feeling an enormous tenderness toward Him.

"I love You, dear God. And I promise to always serve You."

I felt I had just crawled onto His lap, and now He was tucking me in for the night. I was full of love and peace and joy. And those were the feelings that sang me to sleep.

The next morning I awoke, rested, but not quite ready to jump out of bed. He had indeed spoken to me in a dream that night. The "secret place of the Most High" became real to me. I knew what it was like to "rest in the shadow of the Almighty."

To rest.

Not only to strive, but to rest. That's what I had missed out on so much over the past year. I had worked really, really hard. I had believed really, really hard. But I had not rested in God nearly enough.

That night I experienced what it was like to be nested *under* Him. To be covered with *His* feathers. To find refuge under *His* wings.

I wasn't afraid.

I wasn't anxious.

I wasn't ashamed.

I was *His*. His child. His baby bird. And He was going to help me fly. Maybe not today, but someday. I wasn't destined for the nest. I felt destined for the sky. He knew that about me long before I knew it about myself.

I didn't want to get out of bed. I had been embraced in a dream. By Him. Have you ever felt that way? Ever felt that a dream was so good, so beautiful, you didn't want to wake up?

That's how I felt. As if some of heaven had opened and spilled itself onto me. Drenched in love. Like the loving arms of my heavenly Father were embracing me.

"Our Father . . . who art in *heaven*."

Whatever else heaven is, it is where the Light and Love and Life exist at the center of the universe. I felt as if heaven opened, and I saw my Father's face looking down on me. Looking down at me in delight. Loving me unconditionally.

I basked in that. It wasn't because of anything I had done. It wasn't because I had earned it. He just loved me.

Smells from the kitchen made their way into my room. It was a lazy Saturday morning, but Mom was up early as usual, making breakfast. The smell of coffee perking on the stove, bacon crackling in the pan, and French toast. Mmm.

I threw off my covers and followed my nose to the kitchen.

"Morning, Mom."

"Good morning, Dale."

It *was* a good morning.

I sat down and started to eat. A bite, two bites, three. Savoring each one when . . .

. . . a thought—as white and hot and fast as lightning—bolted across my mind.

I walked *out here. Without crutches!*

I raised my pant leg. The swelling had gone down! I was so excited I couldn't take another bite. But I couldn't share my excitement with my mom. This time I wasn't going to make a parade out of my faith. If I was going to do this, I was going to do it differently, quietly, unpretentiously.

Careful not to overdo it, as I had done in the previous weeks, I hopped back to my room on my good leg. I sat on my bed, looking at my ankle, touching it, rubbing it.

For the first time in a year the ankle looked almost normal. The pain was still there, but the swelling was gone. And with the swelling gone, maybe, just maybe, I could squeak by the FAA physical.

I looked at the clock. A little past eight. *A lot to do,* I thought. *Take the physical. Rent a plane. Talk the person I rent it from into letting me fly it. Alone. Could get one from my aeronautics teacher, maybe, at Compton Airport. Fly to Burbank. Take off from Runway 15. That was crucial.*

Quickly I put on a suit and tie, grabbed my crutches, and hopped to the door. I decided not to call ahead to schedule an appointment. On this short notice, they'd probably not see me. I'd just show up and see if the doctor could work me in.

I never appreciated my MGB more than I did that day. It ate up every straightaway; took every turn in stride. Arriving at the office of an FAA medical examiner in Long Beach, I left my crutches inside the car and hopped on my good leg to the entrance, saving my tentative left foot for the exam. I took a deep breath before opening the door.

This is it, I told myself.

I walked through the door, slowly and steadily, trying to walk as normally as possible. It hurt so bad. I limped slightly into the waiting room as I walked to the front desk and asked for an application.

Have you ever had a concussion? the form asked.

Yes, I answered, determined to tell the whole truth.

Have you been hospitalized within the past five years?

Yes.

Have you had surgery within the past five years?

Yes.

Have you at some time lost consciousness?

Yes.

The questions were getting harder, more probing. And then the last question.

Have you ever been the pilot in command at the time of an airplane crash?

No.

Passenger, yes. Pilot, no.

Nervously I handed back the form and prayed under my breath, "God, You have brought me this far . . . would You please allow the paperwork to go through?"

No questions were asked.

The paperwork went through!

Now the physical. The doctor was formal, somewhat impersonal. Another day, another exam. Which, thank God, was cursory. He looked at my head, but he didn't seem to notice the scars. The hair had grown back nicely enough to cover them pretty well.

Whew!

Now the eyes. He looked at both, then examined my good eye, had me read the eye chart. Everything OK there. Now the right eye. And I was praying my heart out between each line. Although I could see pretty well with both eyes, when I closed my good eye, it was quite fuzzy. I could read the larger lines fine, but then came the last line, and I could barely make out the letters.

I knew I could see well enough to fly.

I read the letters the best I could.

Another big but unspoken *Whew!*

"I need you to hop on one leg for two minutes so I can check your heart rate," the doctor said.

"Sure," I said, and you can guess which leg I chose.

The results?

I passed! I walked out of the office with a limp, but I walked out with a First Class medical certificate, dated July 18, 1970.

Under the heading LIMITATIONS, they typed the word *None*.

Later next to that word I typed *Thank GOD!!!!!*

I called my aeronautics professor and asked if I could rent his single-engine Piper Cherokee.

"When?" he asked.

"Now."

UNITED STATES OF AMERICA
DEPARTMENT OF TRANSPORTATION   NO.
FEDERAL AVIATION ADMINISTRATION

MEDICAL CERTIFICATE FIRST **CLASS**

DUPLICATE   10-04-71

THIS CERTIFIES THAT: (FULL NAME AND ADDRESS)

DALE R   BLACK
12102 CHIANTI DRIVE
LOS ALAMITOS,
CALIFORNIA   90720

DATE OF BIRTH	HEIGHT	WEIGHT	HAIR	EYES	SEX
01-01-50	78	170	BRN	BRN	M

has met the medical standards prescribed in Part 67, Federal
Aviation Regulations for this class of Medical Certificate.

LIMITATIONS

None...Thank GOD!!!!!

DATE OF EXAMINATION	EXAMINER'S SERIAL NO.
07-18-70	000540042

EXAMINER
SIGNATURE   *Leslie N. Davis, M.D.*

TYPED NAME A.W. DAVIS, M.D.   4597-35-8

AIRMAN'S SIGNATURE   *Dale R Black*

FAA FORM 8500-9 (1-67)   SUPERSEDES FAA FORM 1004-1

This certificate was acquired exactly one year after the crash. The doctor's office incorrectly typed Dale's height at 78 inches, which went unnoticed until the next year. Dale's actual height is 72 inches

We arranged to meet at Compton Airport, where his four-seater was hangared. I had spoken to him months earlier. Of course he knew about the crash, my injuries, my goals, my faith. I had spoken in his class at the junior college and he had been watching my progress with keen interest and a lot of encouragement.

My MGB ran with the wind and got me to Compton Airport in record time. Mr. Travis, my professor, gave me the customary in-flight exam that was required to prove I was again capable of flying an aircraft and flying it solo.

Once in the air, he had me stall the aircraft several times, take some steep turns, some takeoffs and landings, a complete check ride.

Back on the ground, he had me fill out some rental forms and then he signed my logbook. He looked at it before giving it to me. "Looks like you haven't flown in a while," he said, knowing the full reason why.

"You're right, sir. I've been busy with college. You see, I've got this aeronautics professor . . ." I looked at Mr. Travis, grinning. "He's incredibly demanding."

He smiled back, endorsing my logbook to fly the Piper Cherokee 140 with the words, "Safe to operate PA-28-140 as Pilot in Command. July 18, 1970."

He handed me the book and placed a hand on my shoulder. "Welcome back, Dale."

It felt great to *be* back.

I hopped back to the small plane. My ankle was hurting pretty bad by now. Cleared for takeoff, I taxied to the runway and took off for Burbank. By the time I landed, the pain was severe from using my left foot for braking and my left arm for landing. Even though I was compensating by using my heel only for rudder and braking, my ankle was getting more of a workout than it had in over a year, and it was throbbing.

In spite of the pain, though, I felt great. Captain of my own airplane again.

Moments after landing in Burbank, I was ready to take off again and complete my mission. I taxied to the runway and stopped at the intersection of Runway 15. I picked up the microphone and radioed the control tower.

"Burbank Tower, this is Cherokee 37 November, over."

"37 November, this is Burbank Tower, go ahead."

"Burbank Tower . . . this is 37 November. One year ago today . . ."

I released the mic button, ending the transmission. Overwhelmed with emotion, I lowered my head and cried. I cried so hard I wasn't sure I could go on.

"37 November, this is Burbank Tower, go ahead . . ."

I dried my eyes with my shirtsleeves, then looked around the cabin for something to *keep* them dry.

"37 November, this is Burbank Tower, how do you read?"

I took several deep breaths, yanked off my dress shirt, and blotted my face. *I'm going to fly this flight*, I said to myself. *And I'm going to do it now.*

"Cherokee 37 November, this is Burbank Tower, how do you read?"

I took a deep breath and pressed the button on the mic.

"Burbank Tower, this is Cherokee 37 November. One year ago today a Piper Navajo crashed into the air memorial Portal of the Folded Wings, just south of the airport. Two pilots were killed. I alone survived. I dedicate this anniversary flight to the glory of God."

The tower was silent. I wondered if they had heard me. But they were fighting emotions of their own.

"37 November, stand by."

Another pause, and then the words "37 November, two of us were on duty that day . . . we didn't think anyone survived."

Again a pause.

"37 November, we're glad you made it! Congratulations!"

A fresh flood of emotion washed over me. I was shocked anyone even remembered.

"37 November is requesting to use the full length of runway one-five. Negative intersection departure."

"Roger, 37 November. You're cleared to cross runway one-five. Taxi to the approach end, hold short . . . monitor this frequency."

While holding at the approach end of the runway, I completed the engine run-up . . . once . . . twice . . . three times.

Looking across the airport, I focused on the southern end of the runway.

The air memorial stood indifferently against a hazy sunset sky. I glanced at the runway . . . back to the memorial . . . then to the cockpit instruments. There was nothing else to check.

"Burbank Tower, 37 November, ready for takeoff. I'd like to remain in the pattern."

"Roger, 37 November, you're cleared for takeoff runway one-five. Report right downwind. Have a *very* safe flight."

Suddenly I was terrified. This time I was flying over the monument alone. I paused a moment to regain my composure. *No,* I reminded myself. *I wasn't flying alone. I had never flown alone.* A calm assurance came over me.

I pushed the throttle forward, heard the familiar rev of the engine, felt the power under each wing, the familiar bouncing, and in a moment I was airborne.

My eyes found the huge ornate dome, glinting in the sun, and they fixed on it. With unblinking determination, I stayed the course, taking the same route the Piper Navajo had taken a year earlier. The closer I got, the harder my heart beat. Then, barely a hundred feet over the dome, I passed it.

As it vanished beneath me, tears streamed down my face. I mopped them with my shirt.

That day I took three passes over the Portal of the Folded Wings. As I did, I softly said, "Thank You, God. Thank You. Thank You. Thank You."

When the sun fell below the horizon, I banked toward the airport. I did a touch-and-go landing and radioed for permission to go home.

"Burbank Tower, this is 37 November, requesting a straight out departure."

"37 November, roger. Straight out departure, approved."

A pause, and then the microphone crackled one last time.

"37 November, Burbank Tower. A very . . . big . . . congratulations to you . . . from all of us."

I was so overwhelmed I couldn't speak. More tears. So many tears they seemed to be running not only out of my eyes but out of my nose, my mouth, every pore on my face.

I wanted to say something to them, but I couldn't find the words. I didn't want to give the impression that I alone had accomplished this feat. I knew that if God hadn't reached down and performed a series of miracles on my broken body over the last twelve months I couldn't be flying now. And if God hadn't orchestrated today's new answers to prayer, this anniversary flight as pilot in command never could have taken place. I knew then and have always known since that although I am small, I am connected to a very big God.

As the single-engine plane climbed, my eyes fell on the lush green grasses of the Hollywood Hills Forest Lawn Cemetery, where Chuck was buried. I thought about Chuck and Gene, how they died, and how I should have died along with them. I stared down at St. Joseph Hospital and Dr. Graham's office. I thought of the thirteen surgeries, all the people I had met—the doctors, nurses, friends who came to visit. I remembered Joel Green, who took his own flight to heaven just hours after we met. So much flashed through my mind. And with those images came the words I wanted to say to the men back at the control tower.

"Burbank Tower, thank you for your help today. This is 37 November, reminding you that with God . . . nothing shall be impossible."

⑲

ANNIVERSARY SURPRISE

Once I touched down at Compton Airport, I climbed into my car and headed for home. *How will I tell my parents?* I wondered. How could I find the words to tell them how much this meant to me, why I had to do it? How could I tell them that I wouldn't be going into the family business, that for some reason I was going to fly. I had to fly, had to or something essential would die in me?

How do you say things like that to your mom and dad? How do you speak your heart without breaking theirs? How do you tell them you have to leave the nest? That even though your wings aren't healed you have to stretch them? You're grateful, but you've got to get on with your life. How do you look your mom in the eye and say those things when she knows that every time you get into a plane, you put your life at risk? You risk another crash. Risk hurting her all over again. Risk inflicting a wound that may never heal.

How do you do that?

I didn't know.

I pulled into the driveway, careful how I got out of the car. It had been a long day, and my body felt it. I left my crutches in the car. I wanted to end the day walking through the door on my own two legs.

My steps grew slower the closer I got to the front door, putting off the inevitable as long as possible, steeling myself for their reaction.

I opened the door.

"SURPRISE!"

The house was filled with friends and family. And my mom and dad—whose hearts I feared breaking—had arranged a One-Year Survival Anniversary party. My brothers were there. My college roommate was there. My next-door neighbor. My girlfriend, Anna, and her sister Susan. Gramps. Grandma. Jerry and Verna. The people who had prayed for me. Cried with me. Encouraged me. Visited me. They were all there. All there and cheering me home.

Grandma pulled me to the sofa and snuggled next to me, nuzzling me, holding and rubbing my hands. Mom played the piano. Everyone patted me on the back. Loving me.

It was a bit of heaven, one of the closest I've experienced on earth.

As people were enjoying the festivities, my mother went to the kitchen. I followed her, knowing I had to tell her, knowing she would want to be told.

"Mom, I, uh . . . I need to tell you something."

She braced herself.

"I need to tell you where I was today, what I did."

I paused, looking into her eyes. I was so excited, but I didn't want to hurt her, didn't want her to feel that I was rejecting my home, the family business, everything she and dad had done for me.

"I passed the FAA medical today. I flew over the memorial. And I did it as the command pilot. Three times."

Her face registered shock. She gazed at me for a long time, speechless.

"I'm proud of you, Dale!" Tears fell from her eyes. She gave me a hug, my wilted T-shirt blotting her tears. "I know that was important to you," she said, knowing full well that my choice would take me away from her, possibly forever, possibly leaving a hole in her heart that could never be filled.

She pulled away and wiped her tears, looking at me tenderly.

"I guess you're just destined to fly."

My secret was no longer a secret. She ushered me into the living room and shared it with everyone.

That's when the real party began.

✈

God loved the tenderhearted boy who somewhere along the way to growing up had lost his way. He remembered the boy and the boy's prayers as he knelt beside his bed. He went after the little boy and brought him the last part of the way home.

And the two of us—the boy I once was and the man I had become—knelt together to pray. They prayed about how much the boy needed his Father . . . and how much the man needed him still.

A year before I wanted to be a pilot.

And I wanted it bad.

A year later, I wanted a Father. My heavenly Father.

And I wanted Him bad.

That is the difference between who I was then and who I am now. A boy wanting so badly to be a man. A man wanting so badly to be a boy. A boy who could sit on his Father's lap and just be held.

Psalm 103 says that God has compassion on us the way a father has compassion on his children. The reason? Because He knows our frame and He knows that we are but dust.

My frame had been wrecked, just like the airplane I crashed in. A joint or two had been ground to dust. And with each passing year I feel the earth making its claim on me.

What I felt in the dream that night before my anniversary flight was not a Father's criticism but a Father's compassion.

I felt so whole, so happy, so healed. So loved. So totally and unconditionally loved.

I felt something else too. I felt peace. The peace a child feels when held in the strong arms of his father, seeing the smile on his face, the glint in his eye, and hearing tender words from his lips.

I realize that I was held by those same strong arms the year before when the wings broke and I fell to the ground. God's hand was in all of it in some mysterious way that has taken a lifetime to understand.

Little by little my life would come back to me. It would take several years of recuperation before I would be back to normal. Someday there would be no more wheelchairs. No more crutches. No more braces. No more eye patches.

I would be back on the baseball team too. I was no longer quick enough to play shortstop, so the coach moved me to outfield.

My body came back, a little at a time.

So did my memory.

And so did the little boy.

The little boy who dreamed of flying.

We're all home now. My body, my memory, the boy I once was. At least we're as close to home as we will be this side of heaven.

⑳

INVISIBLE CITY

**SEVENTEEN YEARS LATER
TUESDAY, MAY 22—01:37—12,000 FEET,
SOMEWHERE OVER SOUTHERN ZAMBIA**

"Captain, do you copy that?"

A jolt on my arm from First Officer Steve Holmes snaps me back to reality, my senses flooding with cockpit sights and sounds that demand immediate attention. Suddenly I am again alert with a burst of adrenaline.

"Say it again, Steve?"

"We're established at the Outer Marker, level at one-two thousand. What do you want to do now?"

The tension in Steve's voice is thick and real, and in a nanosecond my mind is again aware that we are streaking across the night sky in our glistening white-and-blue-striped corporate jet somewhere over south central Africa. Having just descended from 41,000 feet, I slow the jet from nearly the speed of sound to just over two hundred knots. Low on reserve fuel, we are established in a holding pattern over what we think—what we hope—is Lusaka International Airport.

For only the second time in my more than twelve thousand hours of flying, the option of diverting to our alternate airport is no longer viable. In my seventeen years of flying hundreds of Christian ministry flights to over fifty countries, many unusual, awesome, and wonderful things have occurred. But never anything like this.

I stare out the window into the darkness. I can't comprehend what I am *not* seeing. In spite of the lack of apparent weather, we aren't seeing anything. No runway, no airport—not even a city—a city of over a million people that should be right below us.

For the first time ever, our long-range navigational instruments are not working at all. The communication radios are out as well. With the short-range navigational aids that do work, we assume we are flying over the capital of Zambia, but nothing is certain.

"Steve, we're going to stay in the holding pattern until I'm ready to shoot this approach."

Chewing on my words, Steve wipes the sweat from his palms.

"OK, fine, but we're not going to be able to stay here long, right?"

"Absolutely, but by staying high and clean earlier, we've got a little more fuel than I thought we would have. Here's what I need now. Confirm again that we're holding over Joppa, the Outer Marker for Lusaka, Zambia. Check the ADF on your RMI and, using your number two radio only, go ahead and triangulate with two remotely located VORs and of course your DME. Make sure you verify, very carefully, the frequencies using the AUDIO IDENT. I want to know if you believe—without doubt—that we're holding over Lusaka."

"You got it."

"I'm going to check my instruments the same way using the number one radio. I'll do the same thing you're doing but independently. Try the COMM radios one last time."

"You know, Dale, we've been checking all those things during the last hour."

"I know, but I still have some doubt about our location. I mean, look outside, Steve. Have you ever seen or heard of anything like this before?"

Steve slowly shakes his head, squeezing the arm of his copilot's chair as he shifts uncomfortably in his seat.

"See, that's my point. I want you to use all three frequencies, approach control, the tower, and emergency one-twenty-one point five. And recycle the transponder; make sure we're squawking 7-7-0-0, the emergency code. Also, don't click just five times, but seven or more times with your MIC button on the tower frequency—just in case the runway lights can be activated that way."

"We've done all that before too, you know."

"Steve, come on, let's work together. Let's do it all again. I want to know we'll be shooting our last approach into a runway environment—not into oblivion, or into that lake . . . what's it called?" I glance again at the navigational charts. "Yeah, Lake Kariba."

My pulse quickens as I scan the instruments while we both go to work twisting dials and penciling marks on charts to calculate our position independently.

Another part of my brain is reflecting on the combination of events that have brought us to this in-flight emergency. Our alternate airport was Livingstone. There we had adequate runway, good elevation, and a good place to RON (Remain Over Night) if necessary. Only thirty minutes' flying time from Lusaka.

We departed Sudan with tanks topped, enough fuel to fly to Lusaka, execute a full approach with a Missed Approach, then fly to Livingstone, our alternate, and then hold for one hour if we needed to. That should have given us adequate fuel reserves. But things started going wrong an hour or so after takeoff. First, we were required to hold over southern Sudan because the air traffic controllers, who don't have radar, got confused. That used twenty-eight minutes of our fuel reserves. Shortly thereafter we lost the first, then a second Global Navigation System. The GNS units help us navigate, with pinpoint accuracy, to anywhere on the globe. Plus they provide invaluable fuel management and winds aloft data. It's highly unusual for either unit to malfunction, but we've lost both and don't know why.

We then flew via Dead Reckoning navigation over Uganda and Rwanda.

We had no permission to land in either place. We still had no reason to believe things would deteriorate any further. But due to the inaccuracies of our limited means of navigation, we had burned nine more minutes of our precious fuel reserves.

Next, we lost total radio communication over Northern Zambia. This, again, made no sense. We have three COMM radios onboard. All indications from the cockpit indicate our radios are working just fine. Still, no one has responded to our calls. Without the GNS systems giving us the jet stream wind information, we lack valuable flight planning data. The high altitude winds, stronger than expected, accounted for consuming another eleven minutes of reserve fuel.

All these factors taken one by one would be relatively minor and normally wouldn't pose a serious threat to the safety of this flight. But combined, they become a viable force against our fuel supply and our flight-planning options. That's exactly how aviation accidents happen. I know all too well. And it's generally not just one factor, but a combination of factors, that cause aircraft accidents.

This most recent factor, certainly not one we had ever considered, was that now flying over the Lusaka area, we cannot see a runway, an airport, or even the lights of the city. The weather report and forecast called for clear skies with visibility of over fifty miles. So why can't we see Lusaka? It's the capital. But there are no lights coming from any direction, not from Lusaka or from any of the three adjacent cities, as far as the eye can see. Through the cockpit window there is only blackness beneath us.

Steve and I compare our findings.

"Captain, I show we're holding at Joppa, directly over Lusaka, Zambia."

"OK, Steve, I concur."

Even though there still exists some disturbing, unanswered questions, we believe we are flying nine miles southeast above Lusaka's International Airport.

Looking down at the fuel gauges, I verify that we have enough fuel for another turn in the holding pattern, plus one full approach, and a little extra. There's not enough fuel for another Missed Approach. There is not enough fuel to fly to an alternate airport. But there is enough for another turn and one slow, deliberate and controlled precision ILS approach into Lusaka. Presuming it is there. It has to be.

"Steve, we'll do one more turn in the hold."

"Are you sure?"

"I am. Steve, you've got the aircraft."

"Roger, I have the controls."

"Steve, I'm going to dim my instrument lights even further. You stay in the hold, level at twelve thousand—use the autopilot."

"May I hand-fly it instead?"

"Negative. Stay on autopilot, and make sure you select and remain on Altitude Hold."

I want to know that we won't unknowingly drift from our safe altitude of twelve thousand feet. I want the assurance that by using the autopilot, if we drift from our assigned altitude, an aural warning horn will sound, and a very bright light in the center of both instrument panels will illuminate. That will alert us that we are not where we need to be.

My mind immediately references one of the aviation accidents I studied. In 1972, an Eastern Airlines L-1011, holding near the Miami International Airport late at night, crashed into the Florida Everglades partially due to both pilots not knowing that the autopilot Altitude Hold function had been inadvertently disengaged. If Steve varies from our altitude, I will hear the audible warning horn, plus Steve will see the Master Warning Light Illumination.

"Steve, I'm going to close my eyes for the next turn."

I grab my uniform jacket from the coatrack and pull it over my head, making it even darker. Allowing my eyes every opportunity to adjust to the utter blackness outside, I'm hoping that in a few moments my dilated pupils will be better able to pick up any small light on the ground that might be visible.

"OK, Dale, turning right heading one-one-zero degrees, level at one-two thousand, speed two-one-zero knots—established in the hold. I'm on autopilot."

Although it takes about thirty minutes for the human eye to fully adjust for maximum night vision, I only have a fraction of that much time. *But five or ten minutes of complete darkness will certainly help. At least, I hope it will.*

After a few minutes I remove my jacket and rub my eyes. I focus outside with the interior cockpit lights at full dim. Moving my eyes side to side, up and down, I strain to allow my peripheral vision to pick up any sort of light. Even the faintest, tiniest light will help.

I jerk forward. "Wait a minute, Steve."

"Do you see something?"

"I think I see something . . . wait. Yeah, it's a light . . . maybe a flashlight . . . maybe a lantern. OK, I just saw another flash of light. It's gone now, but it was a light.

"There is a small light that is still on," I continue, as I stretch and twist my neck, now looking far back through the cockpit's left side window panel. The light is extremely dim and visible only in the periphery. "But I'm satisfied, Steve. We are over land."

We still, however, have no clue as to why we can't see the city.

By switching the fuel selector on the jet's pedestal, I make a quick study of the fuel levels in the Learjet's five tanks. I'm mortified. I try to swallow but can't. My mouth is completely dry. Taking a deep breath while leaning to my right, I speak matter-of-factly. "We will land this Learjet now, Steve—no matter what. If we don't see the airport by two hundred feet above the ground, we'll descend below minimums. Do you understand? Steve, I will descend below minimums."

"Roger, understand. We'll fly below minimums, regardless."

"Correct. I'll land on a street, a field, sand, or anything. And if for some reason we see only water, then I'll spend three minutes searching for land. If we don't see land within three minutes, I'll make a gear-up, controlled landing into the water. Make sure you look for anything. . . . And all outside lights are ON. Landing, RECOG, NAV, and Strobe lights. Make sure all remain on."

Then in a voice just above a whisper, "Be on the lookout for buildings, you know."

My voice is strangely calm, but internally I am almost in shock. I can hardly believe this flight has deteriorated to this nightmarish level.

Steve squirms and shakes his head. "Roger, you've got it."

I crack open the door into the cabin and look back at the passengers, huddled in the center of the cabin, praying as a group. No one looks up, but I overhear one of the prayers.

". . . and Father, we know that if we pray according to Your will, You hear us, and if You hear us, whatever we ask, we know that we already have, in faith, the petitions we asked of You. We thank You, Lord, for a safe landing. Father, use this experience for our good and Your glory."

Then, turning my attention to the passengers in as calm a voice as possible, I speak: "Make sure you guys are strapped in tightly for landing. And please, continue with your prayers, OK?"

Another shot of adrenaline fires through my veins, knowing that the next few minutes will be the most crucial minutes of my life. This is it. There is no turning back now.

"OK, Steve, let's do it."

"Now?"

"Now. I have the flight controls."

"Roger, you've got the controls."

"Give me the Before Landing Checklist."

With sweat pouring down his face, Steve goes into action, performing the checklist and the many duties required of him before landing.

I am once again flying inbound on the electronic beams of the runway's ILS approach. All checklists are now complete. The sleek, glistening jet is in the landing configuration. The flaps are down; the landing gear, down and locked, verified by three green lights. Both engine igniters are ON as they should be, helping prevent possible engine flameout. I double-check everything again, especially that all our outside lights are ON. I want every available light ON to hopefully reflect off of any early sign of the ground or surroundings. I want to see something—sand, pavement, anything. Hopefully not water. Hopefully not a skyscraper.

"A thousand feet above minimums." Again Steve makes first officer callouts as we descend, following both horizontal and vertical electronic guidance to some invisible runway. Still we see nothing but blackness.

"Five hundred feet above minimums."

Moments later . . . "One hundred feet above."

A second passes.

"Minimums, no ground contact. Minimums."

"Can you see anything?"

"Negative."

"Going below minimums, Steve."

"Roger, no contact."

Suddenly, warning tones and commands from the flight instruments scream out from the cockpit speakers overhead: *GLIDE SLOPE, GLIDE SLOPE—PULL UP.*

"Below minimums, one hundred feet below."

"Can you see anything?"

"Negative. No contact."

GLIDE SLOPE, GLIDE SLOPE—PULL UP.

I try hard to ignore the automatic warnings built into our executive jet.

"Leveling at one hundred feet, Steve. Can't go lower. Keep your eyes outside. Advise when you see something."

I can't take my eyes off the instruments; we're too close to the ground. I can't take my eyes away from the cockpit.

"Steve, tell me you see something. We can't stay here, not at this altitude."

"Steve, I need an answer . . . NOW."

153

The instruments scream out again.

GLIDE SLOPE, GLIDE SLOPE—PULL UP.

"Steve!"

Out of the corner of my eye I see that Steve's face is only inches from the windshield, yet he isn't making a sound. The shock of what he *doesn't* see freezes him in place. I feel as if the wind has been knocked out of me.

For a split second I glance outside into the darkness, wince, and hold my breath. Nothing. Complete blackness. Just as quickly I bring my eyes back to the instruments inside the cockpit.

Frozen in disbelief, Steve can barely think, barely speak, barely move.

"Wait! I have contact. Ground contact!" Steve shouts while pointing. "There's a road, a parking lot—straight ahead. Speed one-twenty-nine, V-Ref plus two."

I tear my eyes from the instruments again to see us flying just above the blurring desert. Ahead and barely visible is a paved surface that is as dark as the back side of the moon. There are no familiar lines, numbers, or stripes on the pavement, but there it is, a solid surface, the lights of our jet now shining all over it. Not water, not sand—a solid surface.

Steve winces again and screams, "Abort! Vehicles on the runway. Abort!"

My eyes dart from side to side along the makeshift runway and find it lined with a dozen military vehicles.

"We're landing, Steve."

I don't have the time to look at everything going on outside, but in my split-second view I see military jeeps loaded with soldiers in full battle gear, half-tracks, and other military vehicles. They are scrambling all over the place.

They better get out of the way, I silently demand as I prepare to bring the jet gently onto the solid surface. Still concerned about fuel, I try to assure myself. *Just another few seconds, and we'll be OK.*

I feel the wheels greet the long-awaited surface, transferring the full weight of the jet from the wings to the landing gear. In that instant my fear throttles down with the engines. My index finger flips a small toggle switch, and spoilers rise above the wings. Panels deploy, adding drag and killing much of the remaining lift. With the palm of my hand resting on top of both thrust levers, I smoothly and quickly pull upwards and aft on the reverse thrust levers, and two jet engines scream again into high rpm. The aircraft's frame vibrates and shudders from nose to tail as engine thrust is directed forward, helping slow the jet. A sudden applause erupts behind me, coming from the passengers in the cabin, no doubt expressing their relief and joy at the answer to their prayers.

I try to maintain smoothness in controlling the aircraft, but my concerns for a smooth deceleration dissolve in an instant as Steve points, shouting: "Stop! They've blocked the runway. Emergency stop!"

Abruptly yanking the reverse thrust levers even farther back while slamming on the wheel brakes with my toes, I hear everything loose in the cabin crashing against the closed cockpit door. The Learjet skids to a halt, stopping cold, just a few feet from two combat readied military vehicles, each brimming with soldiers.

Almost in shock, my trembling hand reaches for and sets the parking brake. Instinctively, I study the fuel gauges, curious to know how little fuel remains. An involuntary chill shudders through my body. With adrenaline racing, Steve's eyes and mine lock for a second, then we look away, shaking our heads, neither of us saying a word.

We made it. Thank God, we made it.

I take a deep breath and expel it loudly. As I sit motionless in the cockpit, I am amazed as dozens of tall black fully armed soldiers in battle fatigues scurry into position and surround our aircraft, all wielding rifles that are pointing directly at me. Steve stares in disbelief. In the center and on top of each vehicle is a single-barreled 50-caliber machine gun, each manned by two towering soldiers, again, pointing directly into the cockpit.

My mind is racing for options as I bring the throttles to cut-off, starving the engines of what little fuel remains. Both engines spool down, and finally . . . it's over.

This flight is now at an end.

But as I peer down the barrels of manned rifles and machine guns . . .

I realize another adventure has just begun.

㉑

ADVENTURES OF FAITH

Powerful lights from every direction light up our jet, almost turning the night into day. It feels as if we are on a Hollywood movie set with the lights blaring, the cameras running, and everyone cued for action.

We are on the ground, half a world away from home. But on precious pavement. And no one has been injured—yet. The thought crosses my mind of the tragic irony—to narrowly escape disaster by landing on unlighted pavement in central Africa, only to be machine-gunned to death by soldiers who misunderstand our purpose.

"Take over the aircraft operations, OK? Keep passengers inside and calm. Release the parking brake when the *After Landing Checklist* is done, and caution on battery power."

Steve sits shivering with fear. "What are *you* going to do?"

"Talk. And follow instructions."

"Good luck."

"Thanks. I'll be back."

My heart is racing as I open the top half of the passengers' cabin door and shield my eyes from the intense lights; I notice that the rifles follow me. The twenty-five to thirty soldiers I can see are wielding weapons pointing directly at my heart and head. The soldiers are backlit, and it's hard to see their faces, but it's clear that each vehicle is equipped with enough firepower to start a small war.

As usual I have no planned speech. I simply pray silently as I have done thousands of times before. *God, Your Word says You'll give me the words to speak when needed . . . so give me those words now . . . please.*

I open the lower half of the door and exit the aircraft alone. Dressed in full uniform, I slowly raise my hands, indicating I am unarmed and submissive; I speak so calmly that even I am surprised.

"Please, don't shoot. We are here to help. We bring the love of Jesus Christ, our Lord and Savior, to the African continent."

I have never said anything like that before, and the words just tumble from my lips. I wonder if they've heard me . . . understood me.

What language do they speak here? I ask myself.

Suddenly, a spotlight from one of the military vehicles turns in my direction, jarring and blinding me. Then, in the most official and distinguished use of the English language I have heard since my last visit to London, comes a commanding voice.

"Why did you land at this airport? No one is permitted to land here. This airport is closed."

With my hands still high in the air, I respond, "Sir, I am so sorry to ask this question, believe me, and I'm embarrassed at the same time. But where are we? Is this Lusaka?"

There is a pause. Some of the soldiers look at each other, then look back at me.

His voice booms. "Yes, Lusaka International Airport. The capital of Zambia. This airport is closed to all civilian aircraft. The runway is being repaved. It has been closed for many months."

"Sir," I reply, deferring to his authority, "will you allow me to reach into my left jacket pocket and pull out a simple piece of paper that we believe gave us permission to land here? Sir, I am unarmed and would never try to hurt anyone. We have flown many miles, all the way from America to visit your wonderful country. Maybe we can offer some assistance."

Although no permission is officially granted, I slowly move my right hand into my uniform jacket. The soldiers' rifles follow my every move with eager fingers on the triggers.

"When we left the United States, we were given written permission to land here in Lusaka."

With the flight plan in my hand, I carefully open it, revealing its contents to my captors.

"Walk forward with your hands above your head."

As I do, I become increasingly amazed with each step. I see a sight I will never forget. Approaching the soldiers, I become aware of how small a person I truly am. The soldiers tower over me as if they are part of an NBA team. No one in the group appears less than six and a half feet tall. A couple of them have to be over seven feet.

I focus on the leader of the group, smile at him, and slowly extend my hand. I am relieved as an ever-so-slight smile creeps across his face. Some of the guns are lowered. From somewhere in the crowd a few soldiers chuckle. A couple of dozen soldiers then huddle together and begin to converse. To my relief, the group seems to have relaxed. Then an unexpected announcement from the leader.

"You must all go to jail," we are told. "Now."

"Sir, in all due respect, I am the one responsible for landing here. They"—I point to the passengers in the aircraft—"are not to blame in any way."

"Get everyone off the airplane. Leave your things. You will walk to jail."

"Walk to jail?"

The passengers deplane, and we are ushered on foot down the airport taxiway.

I wonder what awaits us. I assume we will never see the personal belongings we are leaving behind. But I don't care. I am glad to be safe on the ground. Beyond that, I don't know what to expect.

Eventually our walk brings us to the edge of the airport, where a guard tower stands sentry on the perimeter of a barbed-wire fence with searchlights glaring down at us. A few dozen soldiers surround the building, all wearing green woolen uniforms and matching caps with red bands, toting rifles and tugging at taut leashes that hold German shepherds barking and bearing angry teeth. It reminds me of a scene from a World War II movie. Except there are no stunt doubles!

As the soldiers check our passports and luggage, I ask one of them, "Why are there no lights in your city? In fact, the whole country seems to have no lights at night. Why?"

"Our country has security problems. The whole country is blacked out at night."

Nearer to the terminal I see old, rusting vehicles around the buildings that seem to be throwbacks to an earlier, bygone era.

We are told we can't do anything but stay in jail until the general comes the next day to determine our fate. In the meantime, some of the passengers settle into chairs for the night. Others find other places to sit and rest.

The "jail" is actually a guarded terminal building that has been secured and used as a holding area. Many of the soldiers have living quarters in a portion of this same building. We are allowed to mingle and talk to the troops within the confines of the building.

Before long, several of us get acquainted with some of the soldiers. We talk about music, sports, language, where they were born, things like that. Then we meet several of the wives who live on the compound with their soldier husbands. I am six feet tall, and not one woman is shorter than I am. It's surprising. And remarkably, it's fun. Everyone speaks such proper English that at times I'm a little embarrassed at how undignified we Americans sound.

It's amazing. Ever since Joel Green, I haven't had to worry about what to say to people when it comes to spiritual things. I've learned to just smile, listen to God, and answer the questions I am asked.

The whole world is thirsty for unconditional love. Only God can provide that. My job, I've come to learn, is not to provide the water but simply to point the way to the well—the well of Living Water that God offers each of us through a relationship with His Son, Jesus Christ.

My encounter with the soldiers is no different from the one I had with

Joel Green in the hospital bed next to me. The conversations start with a simple introduction. After that all I do is answer questions, pointing the way to the well.

One of the passengers and I walk over to one of the soldiers who is standing alone, guarding the building. "Hello," we say with a smile. "What is your name?"

"Mwelwa."

We shake hands. "My name is Dale. I'm glad to meet you. So, Mwelwa, where were you born?"

"Ndola is where I was born."

"Where is that?"

"A little north of here."

We continue talking, genuinely interested in this man's life. We ask about his family, his interests, and gradually get acquainted with him.

"Mwelwa," I say. "What's the most important thing in your life?"

He seems surprised by my question, and before he answers, I ask him another question: "Do you know Jesus? I mean, He is the most important thing to me, Mwelwa, but do you know Him? Do you know Jesus Christ as your personal Savior?"

"Well, no, I don't think so."

"Mwelwa, if you died tonight—you do know that someday you will die; I will die. Everyone will, right?" He nodded. "So, Mwelwa, if you were to die tonight, do you know for sure that you would spend eternity with God in heaven?"

"No."

"Would you like to know that?"

"Yes. Of course."

"Mwelwa, the Bible says that there is only one way. . . ."

For the next several hours we have one conversation like that after another, soldier after soldier, wife after wife, on into the wee hours of the morning. By dawn almost all the soldiers and their wives have come to Jesus, praying for forgiveness and receiving the free gift of eternal life. Just as with the woman at the well, it all starts with a simple conversation. One thing leads to another, and all things lead to the well where Jesus is waiting with a cup of Living Water.

Countless men and women are gathered around that well in Lusaka, smiling, their hearts full of joy. You can see it in their eyes. It's almost like those I saw gathered at the gate of heaven eighteen years before, awaiting my arrival. This time *I* am at the gate, so to speak, waiting for *them* to arrive, smiling at them, welcoming these new brothers and sisters at the entrance of heaven.

I am awake the entire night, reveling in the wonder of it all. *This* is why we are here. It isn't a mistake. And we aren't in any danger. We are, in fact, in the safest place we can be—the center of God's will. He has led us here, to *these* people whose lives were so parched, whose souls were so thirsty. In this case, though, I didn't so much lead them to the well as He led me to them.

Others in our group, those who are provided blankets, sleep only an hour or two, but as captain, I feel responsible to be vigilant and keep watch. Around ten the next morning, I am approached by a soldier named Robinson. He says the general is in his office and demands to speak with me. I am ushered about two hundred yards away to another building at the airport. I put my tie back on, still wearing my pilot's uniform.

It is not a pleasant meeting. I take some verbal abuse and apologize profusely for landing without permission, even though as far as I am concerned, I did have permission. Once on the ground, though, it is an entirely different story. And so, with a written apology to the government of Zambia, and after paying a moderate fine, I am given permission to refuel and take off.

When I arrive back at the jail I find Steve praying with a member of the mission team. I pause and bow my head as I hear Steve asking God to forgive him of his sins. I listen with great joy as Steve invites Jesus Christ into his heart and life.

Like my grandfather in years past, it is now I who whisper, "Well, praise the Lord."

Steve is wonderfully transformed by the same love that God had shown to the soldiers and their wives. The same love He makes available to all who will believe.

To God, it doesn't matter if you are black or white, Zambian or American, a soldier named Mwelwa or a copilot named Steve. All are one in Christ. And all are now booked on the same flight to heaven.

As we board the plane, I realize I have a "new" copilot. Steve realizes it too. He has seen firsthand the love of God in action. And seeing it, he has decided to experience it for himself. It both fills him and makes him thirsty for more.

For me, Steve's entry into the family of God is just another of the many answers to my prayers. This time watching God turn a co-worker into a brother.

TUESDAY, MAY 22—16:10—LUSAKA, ZAMBIA

As we taxi the 18,500-pound Learjet to the runway, we get through our routine Before Takeoff Checklist and set up all navigation radios. I rev the engines and the airplane shudders to life, eager to take flight. The soldiers on the tarmac wave enthusiastically, sorry to see us go. As we depart "the surly bonds of earth," the hum of the well-tuned engines is heavenly music to my ears.

Leaving the sea of soldiers behind, it reminds me of my return flight from heaven—how quickly I was swept away, how everything grew smaller until at last it was out of sight. Memories of how wonderful it felt to be in heaven, surrounded by such love, flooded my mind. It was a lot like the love we were surrounded by in the Lusaka Airport.

When we got back to the States, we sent Bibles to Mwelwa and the other soldiers and their wives. After all, they were family now.

That family has grown with each one of the hundreds of mission trips we have flown, with each Bible sent, each gospel tract, each showing of the

Jesus film, each clinic we helped build, each shipment of medical supplies we helped deliver.

A Learjet similar to the one flown on Dale's missionary flight to Zambia. Photo taken and provided by Andrei Bezmylov (as seen on *www.airliners.net*).

I glance past the wing for a final glimpse of the Lusaka International Airport, reflecting on my life before that fateful crash so many years ago . . . and my life after it. As the airport becomes a dot on the landscape, above me only clouds, I realize how much I have changed. For me, airplanes were once symbols of status; now they are symbols of service.

How I used to love the thrill of flight then.

Now it is a different thrill that excites me.

Now it is the thrill of seeing the love of God in action, where I can quench my thirst, if only for a moment, with a little sip of heaven.

A sip that fills me and at the same time makes me thirsty for more.

I feel so full. So satisfied.

Thank You, God. Thank You . . .

For sparing my life.

For healing my broken body.

For giving me new dreams.

But most of all, for allowing me the privilege of serving You and experiencing Your love over and over again.

As we level off at 37,000 feet, heading for South Africa, I select autopilot ON.

Turning to Steve, I say, "You know, we're brothers now."

"What? What do you mean?"

"Well, when two people have invited Jesus Christ into their lives, it means that they are both re-born children of God. That makes you and I brothers in Christ."

"Wow, Dale. You know, I don't really have any close family."

"Well, now you have millions of brothers—and millions of sisters—in Christ, all over the world. And Steve, if you only knew of the family that awaits you in heaven . . . I'll explain more later, OK?"

"Yeah, sure. Thanks. And thanks for choosing me for this trip."

"Steve, I honestly believe it was God who picked you for this flight." I put a gentle hand on his shoulder. "I do have a question for you, though."

Straightening his posture, getting ready to assume some new first-officer duty, Steve responds, "Roger, go ahead."

I smile with a light chuckle. "What do you suppose God has in store for us next?"

He grins, "I can't wait to find out . . . *brother* Dale."

✈

✈

AFTERWORD

PORTAL OF THE FOLDED WINGS

The Portal of the Folded Wings is the massive shrine that our twin-engine Piper Navajo hit that fateful morning of July 18, 1969.

The Spanish Mission Revival structure was built in 1924 by American architect Kenneth McDonald Jr. and Italian sculptor Frederico A. Giorgi.

It was designed as the entrance to Valhalla Memorial Park Cemetery, Valhalla being the mythological palace of Odin, the Norse god of slain warriors.

Originally, visitors drove from Valhalla Drive into the cemetery through the arches that led under the rotunda, past three reflection pools and exquisite garden walls. After it was dedicated, the shrine was used for public events from picnics to concerts to radio broadcasts extending well into the 1930s.

The shrine was built to memorialize the passing of aviation's greatest pioneers, from aviators to engineers to inventors.

James Floyd Smith has a plaque there—the person who, in 1918, invented the manually operated parachute for the U.S. Army.

Charles Lindbergh is also remembered there as the person who, in 1927, flew the first solo flight across the Atlantic.

Amelia Earhart has a plaque in the monument as well, the first woman to fly solo across the Atlantic, disappearing in 1937 over the central Pacific, attempting to circumnavigate the globe.

General Billy Mitchell, the American Army general who is regarded as the father of the U.S. Air Force, is likewise remembered there.

Dale Black will also soon have a plaque there.

My achievement? I survived.

I survived in order to dedicate my career to improving aviation safety.

I survived to train scores of professionals to become better and safer pilots.

I survived a crash that took the life of two pilots and caused $70,000 worth of damage to the shrine.

After the first anniversary flight, still haunted by feelings of guilt, wondering if I had in any way been responsible, I tracked down the remains of the plane that had been taken away for salvage. The tail was in Van Nuys. The cockpit and engines were in Long Beach. So was the throttle quadrant. But the pieces of wreckage did nothing to solve the mystery that still haunted me.

I was finally able to retrieve a copy of the FAA accident report, and scoured it for answers. That official report revealed that both fuel selectors were in the ON position at the time of the crash. My feet had *not* turned them off. Also, both engines had been operating at full power on takeoff and on impact, so the problem wasn't with the engines. I pored over the report of the accident, which cited "pilot error" as the cause of the crash.

Several factors contributed to the fatal crash that day. The intersection departure made for an unforgiving takeoff. The plane never increased to the proper speed. Gene had pulled the controls back too quickly and too sharply, lifting off the runway prematurely. The plane momentarily seemed to be airborne due to what is called "ground effect," which is a false feeling of lift created by the plane's proximity to the ground. When you climb to approximately one hundred feet, the ground effect goes away. When Gene noticed he didn't have enough power to keep climbing, he applied full-throttle to the engines. Chuck stepped in, but he was too late. He tried to lower the nose to pick up speed, but it wasn't soon enough to clear the trees. The left wing of our plane clipped the trees at eighty feet, which turned the aircraft just enough for a direct impact into the dome of the mausoleum.

We slammed into the memorial at 135 mph, hitting it just five feet from the top. It was that combination of factors that caused the crash.

The crash was chronicled in all the newspapers in surrounding cities, and I've been told it was later memorialized in *Ripley's Believe It or Not*.

Not quite the epitaph I was hoping for.

The epitaphs of others are noted on tombstones that fill Valhalla like so many tabs on file folders of the fallen.

Aviators are memorialized there, but also athletes like Gorgeous George, the wrestler. And countless actors. From Oliver Hardy of Laurel and Hardy fame to Ruth Robinson, one of the Munchkins in *The Wizard of Oz*. Even the voice of Jiminy Cricket is buried there, Cliff Edwards. Countless others are there, too. Who even remembers their names? Let alone the lives behind the names.

Located in North Hollywood, the cemetery is just off the end of Runway 15 at Burbank Airport, directly in the flight path. Since the opening of the airport, a new entrance to the cemetery was designated. Cars no longer drive through the shrine's arches. An iron fence has been erected around the plaques inside the dome. And the three reflection pools have long since been filled in.

For the first couple of years after the accident, I went to the memorial every chance I got. Sometimes with family or friends, sometimes alone, about every two weeks.

During that time of change in my life, I found a new girlfriend. She looked beyond my broken body and limitations, and loved me for who I was and what I'd become. Her name is Paula, a tall blonde who loves God in an extremely personal way. We were married in 1972.

The last time I revisited the memorial was on July 18, 2009, with Paula. She arranged for a special flight that day. Our daughter, Kara, took pictures as I flew a small single-engine Cessna 172 from the French Valley Airport in Southern California. After the flight, we drove our car to Burbank. We toured Dr. Graham's old office and St. Joseph Hospital, and spent some time at the grave of Chuck Burns. As always, we prayed together at the Portal of the Folded Wings.

I'm not sure why I keep going back. I have no unfinished business there. I have closure now, and peace. But I still return regularly.

I just turned sixty, and the shrine is more than eighty years old. It underwent a facelift in 1994, covering the gaping cracks, replacing the fallen tiles—a poignant reminder of the decay that will make dust of buildings and people alike, in the end.

Architecturally, the shrine lifts our eyes toward the sky, as if to say, "This is not their final resting place."

The remains of fifteen pioneers of aviation are buried within the shrine, from the first dirigible pilot to the machinist who made the Wright brothers the fathers of modern aviation. His plaque reads:

Charles E. Taylor
ASSISTANT TO WRIGHT BROTHERS IN
BUILDING FIRST ENGINE AND
FLYING MACHINE
May 24, 1868–January 30, 1956

My favorite plaque is the one over the remains of the chaplain at the site:

John F. F. Carruthers
AUGUST 31, 1889–JANUARY 13, 1960
CHAPLAIN, PORTAL OF THE FOLDED WINGS
AIR HISTORIAN

AT THE GRAVE, WHEN MY WARFARE IS ENDED
THOUGH NO FLOWERS EMBLAZON THE SOD
MAY A PRAYER MARK THE GOOD I INTENDED
LEAVING ALL DECORATIONS TO GOD.

With more life behind me than ahead of me, I wonder how my memorial will one day read. Not the one someone inscribes on a plaque, but the one my Father God writes.

COMMUNION ON THE MOON

The headlines immediately before and after my crash were all about the Apollo 11 flight. John F. Kennedy's dream of putting an American on the moon was first publicly voiced by the president in 1961, and it was voiced with resolve. His speech left an indelible impression on me. By the end of the decade, he vowed, the U.S. would have a man on the moon. Here we were at the end of the sixties, and it appeared as if that dream was going to come true. After several preliminary missions that put men into orbit around the moon, this was to be the first mission to put them on the moon.

It seems ironic to me that while I was in a coma and visiting the splendors of heaven, astronaut Buzz Aldrin was leading Neil Armstrong and the NASA team in the first official, or maybe not so official, activity on the moon's surface. Buzz conducted Holy Communion. Talk of what they did was hushed for many years but is now public knowledge. Still inside the newly arrived lunar module, Buzz Aldrin believed the best way of showing respect and celebration was to thank God for their safe arrival by acknowledging Him in taking communion as the first human act on the moon's surface. He chose to honor God for this human victory, and he did so against much resistance. In some way, I have felt connected to Buzz Aldrin ever since.

ANNIVERSARY FLIGHTS

Working enormously hard through my injuries, I eventually, and gratefully, became a commercial pilot for TWA. I also became an FAA check airman for the Boeing 737, Learjet, and the Cessna Citation. I spent my career helping train airline pilots and tried my best to improve aviation safety as a ground, simulator, and flight instructor, as well as a flight examiner.

Each year on July 18, for the first twenty-five years, I flew as pilot in command over the Portal of the Folded Wings, with two exceptions. In 1971, I was a volunteer missionary in the jungles of northern Peru. The next year, Paula and I, newly married, returned to those same Peruvian jungles to share the love of God and the gospel message with the Aguaruna Indian tribe. What an experience. But that's another book.

Dr. Graham was a regular passenger for many of my anniversary flights over the years. So was Ron Davis, my best friend and the one most instrumental in me becoming a pilot in the first place. Friends from college or from the family business often joined me, and later other pilots or missionary friends.

On those flights I flew an assortment of airplanes. From the Cherokee 140 to the Cherokee Six, Piper Seneca, Aztec, and of course the Navajo on anniversaries 1977 and 1978. Later I flew the Cessna Citation I, Citation II, the Learjet 24, Learjet 35, MU-2, Piper Cheyenne II, and Learjet 55. Some years I was able to radio the tower and give them my traditional transmission, publicly dedicating the flight to God. Other years the tower appeared too busy, so I didn't attempt the radio announcement.

On the eighth anniversary of the crash, Dale was finally able to fly a Piper Navajo (the same type that crashed) as pilot in command over the Portal of the Folded Wings.

Of all the anniversary flights flown on July 18 over the monument, one is burned in my memory like it happened yesterday. Paula and I had arranged for a small prayer service near the Portal of the Folded Wings, led by our family friend and pastor of my youth. The control tower allowed us to park our jet at the southern end of Runway 15, off to the side. From there the monument and cemetery are close and clearly visible. Our son, Eric, and daughter, Kara, now old enough to comprehend so much more, seemed moved by the experience. Dr. Graham was there, along with several others.

We read from Psalm 91, then prayed and thanked God for answering so many prayers. Next we boarded the twin-engine Learjet that my company managed, this one called *Lady Barbara,* Frank Sinatra's private jet.

As usual, Paula took charge of the passengers and got everyone seated while I taxied the airplane to the approach end of Runway 15. I set the parking brake prior to takeoff.

What is so memorable to me is what happened when I took a peek into the cabin prior to making the traditional call to the control tower. Somehow I connected all the dots again. Dr. Graham's smiling eyes met mine. Here was the man who had helped put my body back together. The man I had seen from outside of my body in the emergency room, the man for whom I was filled with an overwhelming love within minutes of my awaking from the coma, even before I could talk. Dr. Graham winked and gave me a thumbs-up.

I saw the expectant faces of our precious children. If God hadn't spared my life, Eric and Kara wouldn't be there. I remember watching Paula, seeing her so full of God's love and wisdom, as gorgeous as ever, and knowing she'd drop anything, anytime, to obey God. Another happy face that day was my pastor, Mark Smith, who had baptized me when I was twelve years old. I remember the joy, the unity, the peace. But primarily, it is the love I will never forget. It is the love from and for others that reminds me more of heaven than anything else on earth.

Dale and Dr. Graham in a TWA Boeing 747 at Los Angeles International Airport. Photo taken on the tenth anniversary of the crash, July 18, 1979.

I called the tower: "Burbank Tower, on this day in 1969, a Piper Navajo crashed just south of the airport. Two were killed. I alone survived. I dedicate this flight to the glory of God." The throttles were advanced and the jet screamed into the air barely above the monument. As I looked down, I reflected on the familiar Scripture we had just read minutes earlier: "He who dwells in the secret place of the Most High shall abide under the shadow of the Almighty" (Psalm 91:1). The secret place for me was the relationship between my loving heavenly Father and me.

It was an understanding that He and I have. This is because of my uniqueness as His creation, and because of His amazing capacity to love me as a single individual.

And just think . . . if God loves me this way, imagine how much He loves you.

....

For God so loved the world that He gave His only begotten Son, that whoever believes in Him should not perish but have everlasting life. For God did not send His Son into the world to condemn the world, but that the world through Him might be saved. He who believes in Him is not condemned; but he who does not believe is condemned already. . . . —JOHN 3:16–18

....

On the twenty-fifth anniversary, I guess you could say I had a climatic moment. I was able to fly captain in a United Airlines Boeing 747 from Denver to Burbank and back. My son, Eric, was the copilot and my wife, Paula, and daughter, Kara, were able to sit in the cockpit for the entire round-trip flight, right next to the UAL instructor pilot. (Oh, did I mention this was a United Airlines, $120 million Boeing 747-400 six axis flight *simulator*?)

Following the twenty-fifth anniversary flight in the simulator, Paula had arranged for a surprise celebration backyard barbecue. Many friends from the airlines and the local church, plus our children and relatives, were in attendance, and it was a complete surprise to me. During the festivities, Paula came over to me, pointed skyward, and asked, "Dale, what kind of airplane is that?"

I looked up and for once was not exactly sure. But it was circling right above us, so I had time to study it.

"Take a good look, Dale."

"Well, I think it's a uh—uh."

I was so focused on trying to determine the aircraft type, I couldn't see anything else. (Has that ever happened to you? Happens to me a lot.) Then Paula, who knows me so well, said, "Dale. What is the airplane *pulling*?"

Finally I saw it. Behind the aircraft, a large banner read, "Dale— Celebrating 25 years. Praise God!"

My mouth dropped open and my eyes filled with tears.

All I remember next was bowing my head, hugging Paula, and thanking God again for sparing my life.

Dale and Paula on the twenty-fifth anniversary of the crash, 1994, at the United Airlines Training Center in Denver.

DR. GRAHAM—SPECIAL FRIEND

One of the last things Dr. Graham cautioned me about in 1970 was not to injure my left ankle again. Although it was an answer to prayer on so many levels, the blood circulation in the talus bone remained at only 40 percent after two years.

Within a few years, Dr. Graham and I didn't see much of each other. He was busy with a thriving practice as well as traveling the country, giving lectures and attending Evel Knievel's events.

I was still working to regain what I had lost in the accident. Due to the head injuries, my short-term memory had been permanently impaired. For years I studied everything I could on how to improve my memory. I discovered that anything I wanted or needed to learn now had to be placed into my long-term memory, or I simply couldn't recall it. This required an extraordinary amount of study, review, and more review to get things to "stick."

In the midst of this new way of living, I was hard at work in flight training, gaining more aviation certificates and ratings, and busy finishing college; I was now married and raising a family, and also worked full time at the family business to pay for it all.

I've mentioned that before the crash I had been very active as an athlete. Afterward, I returned slowly to a variety of sports. I played softball, swam regularly, played tennis. I even got back to water-skiing, lifting weights, and some boxing. These activities helped me keep my focus on recovery instead of falling into self-pity about the things I couldn't do.

Then one day in 1976, while playing sandlot tackle football, I blew it. I pulled back to throw the pass, but my wide receiver wasn't open (at least that's my story, and I'm sticking to it). I had to run the ball for the first down. A would-be tackler forced me to jump over him. When I landed, I was pretty sure I'd broken my left ankle.

For three months it hurt horribly. I continued to work and acted as normal as possible in public. But at home, I used my old crutches from after the crash. (I still have those crutches, by the way.) Paula tried repeatedly to get me to go see Dr. Graham. For two more months I refused. "It'll be fine," I'd say.

Not only was I in excruciating pain, but I had never told Paula that my ankle was only 40 percent vascularized—that the rest of the ankle bone had no blood circulation and was considered dead.

After her persistence, I finally broke the news to Paula. I also shared about Dr. Graham's warning not to run or jump, and my foolish disregard of the doc's advice.

Paula handled the news amazingly well, but she still encouraged me to see Dr. Graham. He had the talent, the experience, and all my files. He'd know exactly what was wrong and what to do about it.

Finally, five months after the football injury, I conceded. Paula made the appointment, and I went to visit Dr. Graham.

As I sat in the examining room, it was as if I had gone back in time. Seven years after the crash everything was still familiar. When Dr. Graham finally walked in he didn't even say hello or make eye contact. His hands went immediately to my left ankle and he held it warmly, like it was something precious to him.

"What brings you in here today, Dale?"

I explained what had happened.

He took X rays, and a few minutes later we were standing in front of the familiar screen.

Silence.

He said nothing. He didn't even look at me. Then he gazed out the window for a moment, then back to the X rays.

More silence.

It was more than enough time for somebody to say something.

"Doc? What is it?"

"It's normal." He slowly shook his head, rubbed his chin.

"What do you mean?"

"Your ankle is normal."

More silence.

"Doc, you used to talk to me in percentages. You used to say, 20 percent healed, 30 percent, or 40 percent vascularized. So what percentage are you seeing today?"

He paused, looking for the right words.

"Dale, your ankle is *100 percent*. Completely vascularized."

The doctor walked out of the room. I wasn't sure what he was feeling, what it all meant to him.

I borrowed the office phone, called Paula and broke the news. She was amazed and relieved. Together we thanked the Lord.

About ten minutes after my phone call, the doctor came back into the room, composed and warmer this time.

"Dr. Graham, if my ankle is healed, then what is causing all the pain?"

He pointed to the X rays as he spoke in medical terms I couldn't follow. The bottom line was that although my ankle was 100 percent vascularized, many bones inside the ankle needed relief by repositioning. He picked up my shoe and showed me where it was putting pressure on some of the bones in my ankle. He suggested that I get special orthopedic shoes.

He wrote down the name of a podiatrist and had his secretary make an appointment for me. Then he started fashioning a handmade insert with a pair of surgical scissors.

"In the meantime, put this in your left shoe. It'll take some pressure off the talus." Even though I never kept my podiatrist appointment, I did buy some new shoes and kept the insert inside, and the pain slowly faded away. But this whole event seemed to have a wonderful purpose.

About two weeks later, back at our home in Long Beach, we got a call from Dr. Graham. He invited Paula and me to his home for dinner.

Dr. Graham gave us a tour of his luxurious estate, which overlooked the city of Burbank and the San Fernando Valley. I could easily see Hollywood-Burbank Airport, and my eyes gravitated to the newly installed red light on top of the Portal of the Folded Wings.

During our wonderful dinner overlooking the city lights, Dr. Graham showed signs of vulnerability. I had seldom seen this softer side. After dinner we discussed the many miraculous events that he had been witness to throughout the aftermath of the crash. Dr. Graham had a front-row seat, observing a personal, loving God who had revealed himself over and over throughout the days and years following the accident. Ultimately that evening, I was able to share the free gift of pardon made available to us through Jesus Christ. A short time later Dr. Graham surrendered his life to the Lord. His search was over and we became more than doctor and patient. We became brothers in the family of God.

About a month later, back home in Long Beach, another phone call came from Dr. Graham. He wanted me to meet with his photographer at the airport for pictures, and he asked me to dress in my pilot's uniform. I had no clue what he was up to, but I complied. The next day Paula and I met the photographer at the airport, and she took several pictures of me standing in front of different types of airplanes.

A few weeks after that, Dr. Graham's office called, asking me to come in for follow-up X rays. Although surprised, I agreed.

Returning to the familiar office once again, Dr. Graham met me in the waiting room wearing a good-sized smile. Without a word, he grabbed my shoulder and turned me into the hallway past the front reception desk. I shuffled in front of him.

Evel Knievel's framed photo had always been the first portrait in a hallway gallery of celebrities, patients of Dr. Graham. But now, to my complete amazement, my photo hung in that prestigious first position. A large color portrait of yours truly, standing next to a Piper Navajo, hung on the gallery wall.

Needless to say, I was stunned and humbled to be worthy of such an honor.

Then three years later, on July 18, 1979, Dr. Graham and his photographer friend met Paula and me in Los Angeles at my favorite restaurant, the Proud Bird. The aviation-themed restaurant is situated on the approach end of Runway 25 at LAX. The big jets land right in front of you. By then I was a pilot for TWA.

After dinner, we toured TWA's facilities and I showed them the inner workings of the airline. We talked, we laughed, and we fellowshiped.

Although Dr. Graham was my grandfather's age, he and I had become close friends. If you wonder how this could happen, it's because all over the world, every day, people from all ages, nationalities, and races share the most amazing relationship on planet earth. They are one in a bond of love—the love of God flowing among brothers and sisters in Jesus Christ.

The most awesome, glorious experience on earth, next to our

relationship with God through Jesus Christ, is being a part of the family of God.

Only a few months later, just after finishing initial pilot training on the Boeing 707 with TWA, 111 pilots were laid off. I was one of them. This was a huge shock and disappointment.

Due to the fact that I had failed the flight physicals while interviewing with a couple dozen other airlines previously, I couldn't just go fly with another airline. Dr. Graham, knowing this, thought I might be devastated. So he came by to offer encouragement.

"You know, Dale and Paula," he said, "God can use this furlough for good."

I smiled. "You're right, Doc."

"He's done that so many times before. So don't worry about this. You and God, together, you'll bounce back." Now Dr. Graham was the one saying God would take care of it.

The doctor was right. With that furlough came the birth of our jet charter, jet pilot training, and jet aircraft sales company—and a very different future. Years later, I was recalled by TWA.

Dr. Graham has finished his race. I'm so grateful that heaven is his home now. I look forward to our wonderful reunion.

LIVING A DIFFERENT DREAM

Some would say I have lived my dream. I see it a little differently. I did not so much live my own dream as I lived the dream God had when He dreamed of me.

I have flown with Him on over a thousand mission trips, plus the thousands of professional flights. Here and there on those trips I have seen reflections of heaven in the tens of thousands of faces of strangers who became family to me. Brothers and sisters in Christ, so full of love and joy and unity that it seemed like echoes of the love I felt in heaven.

I have experienced so much.

What an adventure!

I tend to think in aviation images. One image that comes back often is the one-year anniversary flight that I described earlier. The words are crystal clear in my memory: "Burbank Tower, this is 37 November, ready for takeoff."

"37 November, roger, you're cleared for takeoff, runway one-five."

A pause, then the words "37 November, this is Burbank Tower. A very . . . big . . . congratulations to you . . . from all of us!"

Tears fill my eyes as I remember my takeoff on that emotional flight. Greater tears come when I realize that the words I most long to hear are not theirs . . . but His: "Well done, good and faithful servant. Enter into the joy of your Lord."

Enter into the joy . . .

For three days in a coma I experienced something of that joy. Both the experience of it then—and the anticipation of it now—have charted the course of my life.

I emerged from that coma to see again . . . walk again . . . fly again.

And most important, to live again.

SIGNING OFF

This is your captain speaking: Before I sign off, I want to thank you for taking this trip with me. May the Lord's protection be upon you wherever you go. Wherever it is, may God go with you. May *He* be your Captain, and *you* the copilot. And when at last your journey is over and it's time for your wings to be folded, know this: Your homecoming will be worth the trip it took to get you there, however bumpy the ride, whatever "crashes" you experience along the way.

Yes, it will be *so* worth it.

You can trust me on that!

HOW THIS BOOK CAME ABOUT

When people find out my husband was the only survivor of a horrific airplane crash and that he also experienced a journey to heaven, they are often curious about how these events have impacted my life and our marriage. They also like to know how this book came about. Let me explain.

Dale and I met at college in Pasadena, California, almost two years after the crash. My dorm mate had a crush on him, and Dale was the one person I heard "all about." He was known as the reformed campus rebel, having been expelled the year before the accident for disciplinary reasons. But due to his remarkably changed life since the crash, college authorities allowed him to return, still in a wheelchair.

Dale was an enigma. He was still a rebel, yet he possessed a strong and tender heart for the things of the Lord. His faith in a God who cared and interacted with him on a personal and intimate level was unique, powerful, and attractive.

A year after we met, Dale and I were married. He continues to be my best friend. We've raised a family together. We've started businesses together. We've traveled the world together. We've experienced wonderful successes as well as severe challenges . . . but always together. For almost forty years we've also ministered side by side. I know him extremely well, and he tells me I'm the only one who truly understands him.

Throughout the years Dale told me several times that he had had an out-of-body experience following the crash. I strongly suspected he had visited heaven, but for some reason he would not talk about it. Why was I suspect? Simple. All the signs were there.

What I didn't know about was Dale's commitment not to share about his journey to heaven with anyone other than his grandfather unless God clearly instructed him otherwise. And when Dale commits to something, he is unbendable.

A few years ago, while Dale was starting to write about his life experiences, we were discussing the moments immediately following the crash. As I had done before, I began to ask probing questions about what he remembered. This time he was unusually quiet. So I asked more questions. He got up and walked around the room. I pressed harder. Suddenly he stood still and silent for several minutes. Then in the greatest emotional response I'd ever seen from him, he let it spill out. He finally revealed to me what I had suspected all along. Dale had visited heaven after all.

As Dale recounted his amazing journey, he paced the floor. I grabbed a pen and paper. He talked. I scribbled notes. This went on and on into the night. The intricate details, the intensity of the concepts, the incredible descriptions . . . I was stunned. His recall was so precise and so completely aligned with the Bible, I knew immediately his experience was not only real but also sacred.

Dale answered each of my questions quickly, but always with great emotion. There were no pauses, no hesitations to his story. His entire awesome journey to heaven was there buried deep in his heart. I was so astounded by his descriptions that at times I froze in place, in awe of what God had revealed to, of all people, my own husband. I have never been more convinced of Dale's honesty and sincerity as when he finally unloaded the secrets of his heavenly journey, the secret he had kept for almost forty years.

For the next several days, hundreds of dots started to connect in my head. So many things I had thought were strange about my husband now made sense. These quirks were, and still are, some of the leftover effects of his heavenly journey.

Dale's values and priorities completely changed after the airplane crash.

That's the primary reason he is dramatically different from anyone I have ever known. He is sensitive toward and strongly drawn to relationships where there is unity and love at the core. Dale doesn't look for facts but the truth in each situation. He sees under the surface of things. He studies the Bible from his heart rather than his head and knows it intimately. Since the crash, he is drawn toward certain types of music. He has a quest to understand order in science, but only to understand more about God. He is fascinated with light and the properties of light as well as space and astronomy. And the list goes on and on. Without question Dale has been profoundly and permanently affected by his visit to heaven.

After much prayer, Dale finally agreed to write about his heavenly journey, but only for immediate family. At the time neither of us dreamed it would ever go beyond that. However, over the next several months, God used a series of events to clearly confirm it was time to share not only about Dale's amazing survival and recovery, but also about his journey to heaven and back.

You should know that his story is verifiable. There are medical records, witnesses, and the lasting results of Dale's changed life. I am probably the best witness to the validity of this story because I've studied the documents and I know almost everyone in this story personally. I still have the X rays, the letters, the newspaper articles, hundreds of photos, the FAA reports, and more. I also know the man. And I, too, have been impacted by the life-changing experience that has affected Dale each and every day of the last four decades.

Due to the injuries sustained in the crash, primarily his difficulty with short-term memory, Dale has had to work enormously hard to accomplish his vocational dreams. But the physical limitations that still challenge him also serve as blessed reminders of his miraculous survival. He's learned several creative "tricks" to compensate for his injuries and, incredibly, has flown for over forty years as a professional pilot following the accident that almost took his life. And probably because of the crash, Dale spent most of his professional career as an award-winning flight instructor and examiner, trying to do his part to improve aviation safety. He is respected by colleagues as one of the best pilot instructors and safest professional aviators in the business.

It has taken a lifetime to more fully reveal God's faithfulness in Dale's life. And that faithfulness has culminated in this book.

I hope you have enjoyed Dale's story and that some part of it has encouraged you in your own journey. God continues to direct our lives, and believe me, after four decades, it is still quite a ride.

—Paula Black